# First Workshop on Dataset Creation for Lower-Resourced Languages (DCLRL 2022)



Held at LREC 2022

Marseille, France
20 – 25 June 2022

**Editors:**

**Jonne Saleva**
**Constantine Lignos**

ISBN: 978-1-7138-6117-1

**Printed from e-media with permission by:**

Curran Associates, Inc.
57 Morehouse Lane
Red Hook, NY 12571

**Some format issues inherent in the e-media version may also appear in this print version.**



Association for Computational Linguistics
209 N. Eighth Street
Stroudsburg, Pennsylvania 18360

Phone: 1-570-476-8006
Fax: 1-570-476-0860

acl@aclweb.org

**Additional copies of this publication are available from:**

Curran Associates, Inc.
57 Morehouse Lane
Red Hook, NY 12571 USA
Phone: 845-758-0400
Fax: 845-758-2633
Email: curran@proceedings.com
Web: www.proceedings.com

LREC 2022 Workshop
Language Resources and Evaluation Conference
20-25 June 2022

# First Workshop on Dataset Creation for Lower-Resourced Languages (DCLRL)

# PROCEEDINGS

Editors: Jonne Sälevä, Constantine Lignos

# Proceedings of the First Workshop on Dataset Creation for Lower-Resourced Languages (DCLRL 2022)

Edited by: Jonne Sälevä and Constantine Lignos

**For more information:**
European Language Resources Association (ELRA)
9 rue des Cordelières
75013, Paris
France
http://www.elra.info
Email: lrec@elda.org

# Message from the Organizers

This volume documents the Proceedings of the First Workshop on Dataset Creation for Lower-Resource Languages (DCLRL), held on June 24th, 2022 as part of the 13th Language Resources and Evaluation Conference (LREC 2022).

In recent years, there has been a significant increase in interest in developing datasets for lower-resourced languages (LRLs) and a greater involvement of the communities speaking those languages in the process. Developing resources for languages that have had fewer resources created for them poses a unique set of technical and ethical challenges that differs from higher-resourced language work.

The overall goal of this workshop was to create a new venue where previously disjoint research communities working on different areas surrounding lower-resourced languages can come together and share their insights across specialized research niches. We endorsed an open and intersectional perspective to the definition of a "lower-resourced language," acknowledging that this designation is both imperfect and often the result of many contributing factors. Our workshop was designed to be open and inclusive, presenting great scholarship from as many different perspectives as possible.

Papers submitted to the workshop were expected to generally revolve around resource creation for lower-resourced languages, but could be fairly broad in scope. For example, we welcomed submissions describing both finished or ongoing research projects, downloadable resources, and position papers containing insights on resource creation for lower-resourced languages that the broader community could benefit from.

The submissions that we received led us to slightly broaden the scope of the workshop to also welcome work in what might be termed *lower-resourced domains*; domains and tasks that are in need of more or higher quality datasets, even if these datasets are not necessarily created in languages that might be considered lower-resourced. We encourage organizers of future workshops and conferences to explicitly include this type of work in their calls for papers.

We are delighted to publish the ten papers that appear in the proceedings of our workshop, and we hope you will find them both informative and thought-provoking. We want to acknowledge that this workshop is of smaller scope than we had originally planned. Like many other workshops and conferences this year, our organizing process was affected by a number of external factors. Chief among them were the effects of the COVID-19 pandemic. Beyond the health and safety considerations, the pandemic has impacted the costs and logistics of conference travel and created additional workload and burnout in the research community.

We found ourselves carrying an exceptional workload from our university in this exceptional time, and therefore we opted to have only a minimal set of organizers and keep the workshop small and focused. We would like to acknowledge and thank the researchers with whom we had originally discussed the proposal for this workshop: David Adelani, Ximena Gutierrez-Vasques, Mmanape Hlungwane, Vukosi Marivate, and Priscilla Tyulu. We hope that in future iterations, we are able to engage an even broader portion of the community and increase the scale of this workshop.

**Organizers**

Constantine Lignos
Chester Palen-Michel
Jonne Sälevä

**Program Committee**

Linda Achilles
Petra Bago
Steven Bedrick
Stergios Chatzikyriakidis
Aparna Dutta
Hafsteinn Einarsson
Steinunn Rut Friðriksdóttir
Imane Guellil
Rejwanul Haque
Asha Hegde
Chaak-ming Lau
Jackson Lee
Muxuan Liu
Alex Lưu
Vukosi Marivate
Malte Ollmann
Hilary Prichard
Karthika Ranganathan
Caitlin Richter
Hosahalli Lakshmaiah Shashirekha
Ridouane Tachicart

# Table of Contents

*Proceedings of the 1st Workshop on Dataset Creation for Lower-Resourced Languages (DCLRL) @LREC2022*, pages 1–9
Marseille, 24 June 2022


# SyntAct: A Synthesized Database of Basic Emotions

**Felix Burkhardt**[1], **Florian Eyben**[1], **Björn W. Schuller** [1,2,3]
[1]audEERING GmbH, [2]University of Augsburg, [3]Imperial College London
Germany, Germany, UK
{fburkhardt, fe, bs}@audeering.com

**Abstract**

Speech emotion recognition is in the focus of research since several decades and has many applications. One problem is sparse data for supervised learning. One way to tackle this problem is the synthesis of data with emotion-simulating speech synthesis approaches. We present a synthesized database of five basic emotions and neutral expression based on rule-based manipulation for a diphone synthesizer which we release to the public. The database has been validated in several machine learning experiments as a training set to detect emotional expression from natural speech data. The scripts to generate such a database have been made open source and could be used to aid speech emotion recognition for a low resourced language, as MBROLA supports 35 languages.

**Keywords:** emotional, database, synthetic, speech synthesis, simulation

## 1. Introduction

The recognition of affect in speech is quite an old research field that gains momentum with the spread of vocal interfaces as numerous applications appear. Examples are natural human machine interaction, gaming and the security domain. The overwhelming majority of approaches to machine learning is still based on supervised learning, which is even stronger for emotional arousal as there is no clear definition, compared to other speech features like speaker age or textual contents. Obviously, labeling emotional data manually is costly and methods to multiply existent data are needed.

With the dawn of modern deep learning based speech synthesizers, emotional expression is usually learned with the data, see Section 2 for some references.

About a decade ago, we have chosen a different approach by simulating emotional arousal with manually adapted prosody rules. In (Schuller and Burkhardt, 2010; Schuller et al., 2012), we already tried successfully to add the synthesized samples to the training of emotional recognition models.

We now re-synthesized five emotional categories plus neutral versions and published them to the research community. We call the database "SyntAct" because it displays basic emotions with always the same prosodic expression, like a bad actor would do.

This paper describes the process of generation of the samples in Section 3, the format of the database in Section 4, and an evaluation experiment in Section 5.

Contributions of this paper are:

- We introduce a new dataset of simulated emotional expression that is available to the public.
- The simulation is based on rules that can target specific emotions.
- We release the scripts that generate the database as well so researchers can extend the data as needed.
- We evaluate the database with respect to its usefulness to train a machine learning model to detect prototypical emotional categories in natural data.

## 2. Related Work

The idea to synthesize training data is not a new one. Based on an existing training database, with deep learning techniques like variational autoencoders (VAEs) (Baird et al., 2019; Deng et al., 2014; Deng et al., 2013) or generative adversarial networks (GANs) (Latif et al., 2020; Eskimez et al., 2020), the generation of new training data has been realised. In some of these approaches only non-audible acoustic parameters have been generated, in other ones, actual speech samples (though not necessarily with semantic content).

An alternative approach is to generate new training data from scratch with traditional speech synthesis approaches. In (Baird et al., 2018), we investigated the likability and human likeness of synthesized speech in general and found that many systems are acceptable.

The approaches to synthesize speech can be categorized like this:

- articulatory synthesis
- formant synthesis
- diphone synthesis
- non-uniform unit selection synthesis
- HMM based synthesis
- deep learning based synthesis

in the order of historic importance. Basically, there has been a trade-off between flexibility and naturalness for the algorithms. While formant synthesis for example is quite flexible with respect to signal manipulation, for the non-uniform unit-selection approach, all envisaged emotional expression must already be contained in the training database. The highest quality of speech synthesizes approaches (with respect to out-of-domain naturalness) are these days based on artificial neural networks (ANN) under the label deep learning (DL) (Zhou et al., 2020). Although these DL based systems deliver very natural speech, it is difficult to determine which emotional expression will be simulated, as they usually are generated by manipulation of the latent space inside the network.

## 3. Preparing the Speech Samples

The synthesised database consists of samples that were generated with the rule-based emotion simulation software "Emofilt" (Burkhardt, 2005). It utilises the diphone speech synthesiser MBROLA (Dutoit et al., 1996) to generate a wave form from a phonetic description (SAMPA symbols with duration values and fundamental frequency contours) and the MARY text-to-speech (TTS) system (Schröder and Trouvain, 2003) to generate the neutral phonetic description from text. Emofilt acts as a filter in between to 'emotionalise' the neutral phonetic description; the rules are based on a literature research described in (Burkhardt, 2000). All six available German MBROLA voices – *de2*, *de4*, and *de7* as female, and *de1*, *de3*, and *de6* as male – were used.

### 3.1. Text Material

With respect to emotional speech, usually three kinds of texts are distinguished:

- Emotional texts, where the emotion is also expressed in the words. This happens often in real world conversations.
- Mundane texts, where strong emotions seem inappropriate.
- Emotional arbitrary texts , that might indicate an emotional event but it's not clear which emotion.

For the experiment at hand, the intention is to soften the problem of limited prosodic variability with a large number of different texts. Therefore we utilized a German news corpus from the University of Leipzig[1] (Goldhahn et al., 2012). No special preprocessing was applied.
The following lists three sentences (in the original language: German).

```
1) Um die in jeder Hinsicht zufrieden
  zustellen , tueftelt er einen Weg
  aus , sinnlose Buerokratie wie Laden-
  schlussgesetz und Nachtbackverbot
  auszutricksen .
2) Um die gesamte Insel zu erkunden ,
  empfiehlt es sich , ein Auto zu mieten .
3) Sowohl die Landesregierung als
   auch die Kreise tragen Schuld .
```

### 3.2. Rule-Based Emotion Simulation

Emofilt differentiates four different kinds of acoustic features:

- Intonation: Here, we model intonation contours that can be specified for the whole phrase or for specific kinds of stressed syllables, with a special treatment of the last one.
- Duration: General duration as well as duration on syllable (differentiated for stress type) and phoneme level can be specified.
- Voice quality: Although voice quality is inherently fixed for diphone synthesis, some databases have voice quality variants (Schröder and Grice, 2003). In addition, a simulation of jitter is achieved by shifting alternating F0 values.
- Articulation: Because with diphone synthesis a manipulation of format tracks is not directly possible, we achieve a simulation of articulatory effort by substituting tense with lax vowels in stressed syllables and vice versa, following an idea by (Cahn, 2000).

The exact values that we decided upon to generate the samples per emotion are detailed in the following subsections.
The scripts to generate such a database have been made open source and could be used to aid speech emotion recognition for a low resourced language, as MBROLA supports 35 languages[2]. It must be noted though, that many MBROLA languages miss implementations of a natural language processing (NLP) component which means that "emotionally neutral" input samples would have to be specified in the native phonetic MBROLA format. Also, for most languages, only two or even only one voice has been made publicly available.

#### 3.2.1. Simulation of Sadness

We applied the following configuration to simulate sadness:

```
<pitch>
 <variability rate="80" />
 <f0Range rate="80" />
 <contourFocusstress rate="30"
   type="straight" />
 <lastSylContour rate="10"
   type="rise" />
 </pitch>
<phonation>
 <jitter rate="10" />
 <vocalEffort effort="soft" />
</phonation>
<duration>
 <speechRate rate="140" />
</duration>
```

[1]https://wortschatz.uni-leipzig.de; we used the list "deu_news_1995_10K-sentences.txt".

[2]https://github.com/felixbur/syntAct

```
<articulation>
 <vowelTarget
    target="undershoot" />
</articulation>
```

This means that the variability of F0 in general has been reduced to 80 %, the F0 contour of the stressed syllables is now straight and the last syllable rises by 10 %. The F0 range has also been reduced by 20 %. With respect to phoneme duration, the speech rate (syllable per second) has been made slower by 40 %. The voice quality has been set to soft vocal effort, meaning that the respective samples from voices "de6" and "de7" were used.

#### 3.2.2. Simulation of Happiness

We decided on the following configuration to simulate happiness:

```
<pitch>
 <f0Mean rate="120" />
 <f0Range rate="130" />
 <contourFocusstress rate="40"
    type="rise" />
 <levelFocusstress rate="110" />
</pitch>
<duration>
 <durVLFric rate="150" />
 <speechRate rate="70" />
 <durVowel rate="130" />
</duration>
<phonation>
<vocalEffort effort="loud" />
</phonation>
```

We enlarge the F0 range by 30 % and raise the whole contour by 20%. The stressed syllables are raised by additional 10 %. The stressed syllables gets an upward pitch direction by 10 %. The speech rate gets faster by 30 % in general, but voiceless fricatives and vowels get an extra speed accelerator by 50 and 30 % respectively. The vocal effort gets stronger.

#### 3.2.3. Simulation of Anger

We applied the following configuration to simulate anger:

```
<pitch>
 <f0Range rate="140" />
 <levelFocusStress rate="130" />
 <variability rate="130" />
 <contourFocusstress rate="10"
     type="fall" />
 <levelFocusstress rate="130" />
</pitch>
<duration>
<durVowel rate="70" />
 <speechRate rate="70" />
 <durationFocusstressedSyls
    rate="130" />
</duration>
<phonation>
 <vocalEffort effort="loud" />
 <jitter rate="2" />
</phonation>
<articulation>
 <vowelTarget target="overshoot" />
</articulation>
```

To simulate anger the F0 range is compressed by 20 %, the contour of the stressed syllables gets a downwards direction and they are raised by 30 %. The speech is made faster by 30 % for all non-stressed syllables whereas the stressed syllables are made longer by 30 %. In addition we apply jitter simulation and the "loud" phonation type.

#### 3.2.4. Simulation of Fear

Additionally, we simulated two emotional states that were discussed in (Burkhardt, 2000), though we did not test them against real databases within the work reported here.

```
<pitch>
 <phraseContour rate="10"
     type="rise" />
 <contourFocusstress rate="10"
   type="straight" />
 <lastSylContour rate="10"
     type="rise" />
 <f0Mean rate="200" />
</pitch>
<duration>
 <speechRate rate="70" />
 <durationFocusstressedSyls
     rate="80"/>
 <durPause rate="200" />
</duration>
<phonation>
 <jitter rate="5" />
 <vocalEffort effort="loud" />
</phonation>
<articulation>
 <vowelTarget target="undershoot" />
</articulation>
```

Fear is characterized by a rising phrase pitch contour, straight stressed syllables and an additional rise at the end. The speech rate is faster, especially for the stressed syllables and the duration of pauses longer. The articulation vowel target is undershot, meaning that stressed vowels get replaced by unstressed ones.

#### 3.2.5. Simulation of Boredom

The second additional emotion we simulate is boredom.

```
<pitch>
 <f0Mean rate="120" />
 <phraseContour rate="40"
     type="fall" />
</pitch>
```

```
<duration>
  <speechRate rate="120" />
  <durationFocusstressedSyls
      rate="120" />
</duration>
<phonation>
  <vocalEffort effort="soft" />
</phonation>
```

Boredom has primarily a falling pitch contour, a slower speech rate, especially with the stressed syllables, and a soft vocal effort.

## 4. Description of the Database

The database is downloadable[3] as a zip file. The format of the data is in the audformat style being described in the next section.

### 4.1. The audformat Package

*audformat*[4] defines an open format for storing media data, such as audio or video, together with corresponding annotations. The format was designed to be universal enough to be applicable to as many use cases as possible, yet simple enough to be understood easily by a human and parsed efficiently by a machine.
A database in *audformat* consists of a header, which stores information about the database (source, author, language, etc.), the type of media (sampling rate, bit depth, etc.), the raters (age, mother tongue, etc.), the schemes (numerical, categories, text, etc.), and the splits (train, test, etc.). It also keeps reference of all tables that belong to the database, which hold the actual annotations and are stored in separate files in text and/or binary format.
A corresponding Python implementation[5] provides tools to access the data, create statistics, merge annotations, and search / filter information.

### 4.2. Specifics of the Database

We generated in total 6000 samples with different textual content, for all six German voices (de1, de2, de3, de4, de6, de7) and each emotion. There are two reasons why not all combinations could be synthesized:

- For some phrases and emotions, the modifications led to the total elimination of phonemes and the result did not adhere to the phonotactics of the voice.
- In some cases, the MARY software, being used to generate the "neutral" phoneme version, ignored the phonotactics of the MBROLA voices.

[3]as zip file and from Zenodo https://doi.org/10.5281/zenodo.6573016

[4]https://audeering.github.io/audformat/

[5]https://pypi.org/project/audformat/

Figure 1: Frequencies of emotions per voice in the database

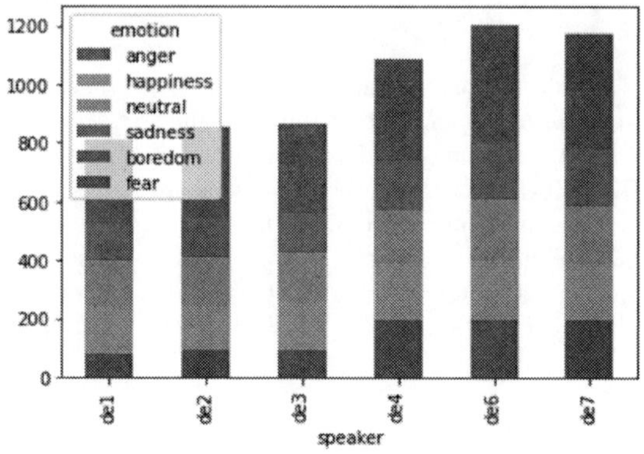


Both lead to an MBROLA error and no samples were generated. The resulting number of samples per emotion and synthetic voice in the database are shown in Figure 1. As can be seen especially the anger and fear emotions caused problems with the voices de1, de2 and de3, probably due to missing phoneme inventory caused by phoneme elisions.
Figure 2 shows a t-SNE plot (van der Maaten and Hinton, 2008) for the eGeMAPS (Eyben et al., 2015) features, colored by intended emotion. As can be seen by the colored clustered, the emotions can be separated based on acoustic features.

Figure 2: t-SNE plot for egemaps featues colored by emotion label

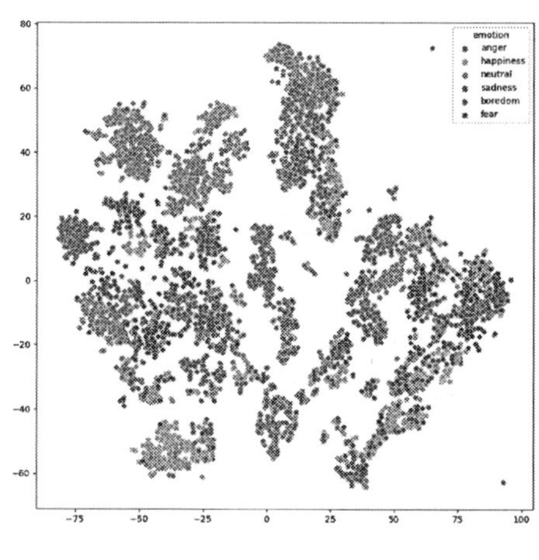


## 5. Evaluation

With respect to evaluation two approaches make sense:

- Evaluate the validity of the emotional expression by a human perception experiment.

| neutral | happiness | sadness | anger | mean |
|---|---|---|---|---|
| .6 | .35 | .5 | .55 | .5 |

Table 1: Results (total accuracy over all labels) per emotion in the perception experiment.

- Evaluate the usefulness with respect to machine learning as a training set.

### 5.1. Perception Experiment

We conducted a perception experiment after we defined the modification rules as described in the literature (Burkhardt, 2000, chapter 5, pages 97-105) . It was a forced choice listening experiment with 20 participants who listened to the stimuli in random order. The results are displayed in Table 1. All emotions were recognized well above chance, the rather low value for happiness is mainly due to the fact that it was often confused with anger. This confusion is often seen in the literature (Yildirim et al., 2004) and caused by a similar level of arousal.
Interestingly, the mean accuracy for all emotions in this perception experiment for the rule-based simulation was highest compared to four others that used prosody copy from actors of the Berlin emotional database (Burkhardt et al., 2005).

### 5.2. Evaluation Databases

We investigate the usefulness of the data as a training set for machine classifiers by setting up a series of experiments with databases displaying acted basic emotions. Although these emotion expressions appear rarely in the real world, its detection still might be of practical value, as for example in Gaming scenarios or to teach children in the autism spectrum (Burkhardt et al., 2019).

Figure 3: Overview of databases with respect to basic emotion portrays

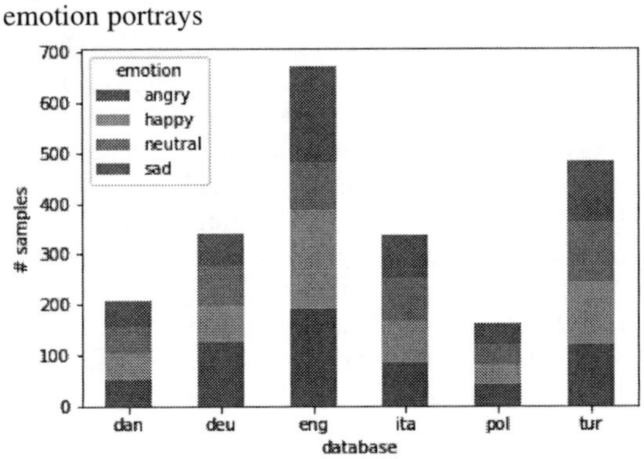


We look at the following six databases from different countries:

- 'emodb' (Germany): The Berlin Emotional Speech Database (emodb)[6] (Burkhardt et al., 2005) is a well known studio recorded dataset.
- 'emovo' (Italy): Italian Emotional Speech EMOVO[7] (Costantini et al., 2014) is a database consisting of the voices of six actors (three female, three male) who utter 14 Italian sentences simulating seven emotional states: anger, disgust, fear, joy, neutral, sadness, and surprise.
- 'ravdess' (USA): The Ryerson Audio-Visual Database of Emotional Speech and Song (ravdess)[8] (Livingstone and Russo, 2018) contains recordings of 24 professional actors (12 female, 12 male), vocalising two English statements in a neutral North American accent. We excluded the songs.
- 'polish' (Poland): The Database of Polish Emotional Speech (Powroźnik, 2017) consists of speech from eight actors (four female, four male). Each speaker utters five different sentences with six types of emotional state: anger, boredom, fear, joy, neutral, and sadness.
- 'des' (Denmark): The Danish Emotional Speech (des) (Engberg et al., 1997) database comprises acted emotions of four professional actors – two males and two females – for five emotional states: anger, happiness, neutral, sadness, and surprise.
- 'busim' (Turkey): For the Turkish Emotional Database (busim) (Kaya et al., 2014), eleven amateur actors (eight female, three male) provided eleven Turkish sentences with emotionally neutral content.

An overview of the databases is provided in Table 5.2. We tested these databases with a subset of the synthesized data being used solely as training. Therefore, all database emotion designations were mapped to the four target emotions of SyntAct, or removed if not part of the four target emotions. The resulting distributions per emotion category can be seen in Figure 3. For the four target emotions (angry, happy, neutral, and sad), out of the 1000 samples per speaker we selected randomly 30 samples per speaker and emotion, getting 720 samples with distinct texts.
We realize that emotional expression is culture and language specific (Neumann and Vu, 2018; Feraru et al., 2015; Burkhardt et al., 2006; Scherer et al., 1999) but as the expression of "basic, full-blown emotions" also is culturally universal and the acoustic feature set that we used for the evaluation does not model linguistics, we think it's justified to use this German data to train

[6]https://www.tu.berlin/go22879/
[7]http://voice.fub.it/EMOVO
[8]https://doi.org/10.5281/zenodo.1188975

| Name | Language | Year | #speakers | #emotions | #sentences | #samples |
|---|---|---|---|---|---|---|
| emodb | German | 1999 | 10 | 7 | 10 | 484 |
| emovo | Italian | 2014 | 6 | 7 | 14 | 588 |
| ravdess | N.-A. English | 2018 | 24 | 8 | 2 | 1 440 |
| Polish Emotional Speech | Polish | 2014 | 8 | 6 | 5 | 240 |
| des | Danish | 1997 | 4 | 5 | 13 | 260 |
| busim | Turkish | 2014 | 11 | 4 | 11 | 484 |

Table 2: Overview of the emotional speech databases

| busim | danish | emodb | emovo | polish | ravdess |
|---|---|---|---|---|---|
| .314 | .317 | .508 | .360 | .381 | .366 |

Table 3: Results in UAR (unweighted average recall) per database when the synthesized data is being used as a training.

an emotion recognition classifier at least for European languages.
For the experiments we employed the Nkululeko framework[9] (Burkhardt et al., 2022) with an XGBoost classifier[10] (Chen and Guestrin, 2016) with the default meta parameters ($eta = 0.3$, $max\_depth = 6$, $subsample = 1$). This classifier is basically a very sophisticated algorithm based on classification trees and has been working quite well in many of our experiments (Burkhardt et al., 2021).
As acoustic features, we used the eGeMAPS set (Eyben et al., 2015), an expert set of 88 acoustic features for the openSMILE feature extractor (Eyben et al., 2010) that were optimised to work well to explain speaker characteristics and in particular emotions. These features are being used in numerous articles in the literature as baseline features (e. g., (Ringeval et al., 2018; Schuller et al., 2016)) as they work reasonably well with many tasks and are easy to handle for most classifiers based on their small number.

### 5.3. Results

In Figure 4 and Table 3, we present the result of our experiment. Note that in the figure, we use the F1 measure as a combination of recall and precision (because the results stand for one specific emotion), while in the table, we report unweighted average recall (UAR, which is the standard measure of the Interspeech Computational Paralinguistics Challenge).
Following the numbers in the table, we can see that all the values are above the chance level (of .25 UAR for four emotions). Likewise, it seems that in general it is

[9]https://github.com/felixbur/nkululeko/

[10]Actually using the Python XGBoost package: https://xgboost.readthedocs.io/

Figure 4: Overview of results per emotion for databases as F1 values

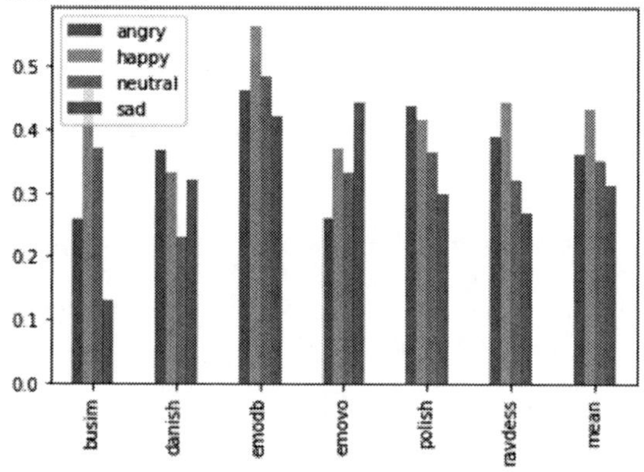


possible to detect emotional arousal with the database for several languages, but considering the results for the specific emotions in the figure, it is striking that the results depend extremely on which emotion is classified in which database. For example, while the simulation of sadness does work quite well fort the Italian database (emovo), this is not at all true for the Polish, the ravdess (American English), and especially the busim (Turkish) databases. On average, happiness simulation result in a much better model than sadness. The German database shows the best performance and it is probably not by chance that the database is also German. Although we did not use linguistic features, the expression of emotions is influenced by culture (Scherer et al., 1999; Burkhardt et al., 2006; Barrett et al., 2019)..
As an example, we present in Figure 5 the confusion matrix for the Emodb database as a test set. As can be seen, the classification mainly worked, especially well for happiness, which is in general the best working simulation based on Figure 4. "Angry" was often confused with happy, which is a quite typical confusion based on a similar level of arousal, but also with sadness, which we can't explain really. "Neutral" was sometimes confused with sadness, and "sadness" consequently with "neutral", probably based on the common low level of arousal.

Figure 5: Example confusion matrix for Emodb database (German) as a test set

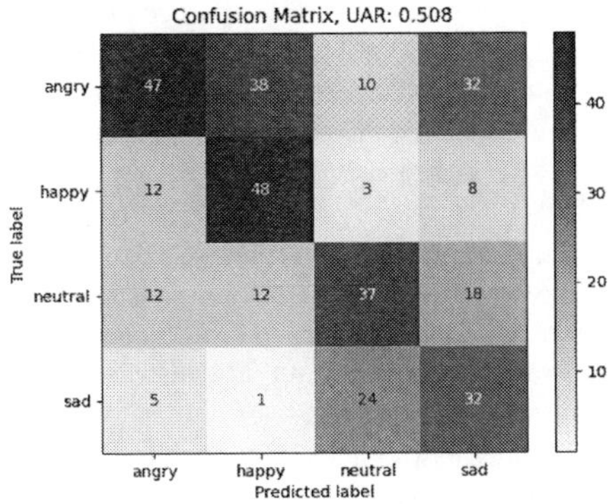


## 6. Ethical Considerations and Broader Impact

With respect to ethical considerations, generally it must be stated that the processing of emotional states is of great severity (Batliner et al., 2022). It should be made transparent to users of such technology that the attribution of emotional states based on human signals by machines based on statistics and pattern recognition is simply a substitute technology, as the true emotional state can never be inferred by others. It is a large part of human-human communication and also human-machine communication benefits, but severe decisions, that affect users well-being, should definitely not be based on this.

Nonetheless, we do believe that the interpretation of the emotional channel is important for natural human-machine speech communication and hope, as stated above, that especially lower resourced languages might benefit from the idea to train emotion aware systems with simulated prosodic variation, which comes cheap and does not require much data.

## 7. Conclusion and Outlook

We described a database of prototypical emotional expression in German that has been synthesized with rule-based speaking style modifications and made accessible to the public. The application of this data to generate a training set for natural emotional expression has been investigated with six international databases.

With respect to the 35 languages the MBROLA supports, we plan to extend the database in the future. Also the number of emotion portrayals may be extended.

A very interesting approach would be the simulation of emotional dimensions like pleasure, arousal, and dominance because on the one hand, many natural databases have been annotated with these dimensions (Lotfian and Busso, 2017), and on the other hand, the dimensions might be mapped flexible to specific categories, like for example "interest". At the time of writing, a first implementation of rule-based independent arousal and valence simulation has already been implemented and awaits evaluation experiments.

## 8. Acknowledgements

This research has been partly funded by the European EASIER (Intelligent Automatic Sign Language Translation) project (Grant Agreement number: 101016982).

## 9. Bibliographical References

Baird, A., Parada-Cabaleiro, E., Hantke, S., Burkhardt, F., Cummins, N., and Schuller, B. (2018). The perception and analysis of the likeability and human likeness of synthesized speech. pages 2863–2867, 09.

Baird, A., Amiriparian, S., and Schuller, B. (2019). Can deep generative audio be emotional? towards an approach for personalised emotional audio generation. pages 1–5, 09.

Barrett, L. F., Adolphs, R., Marsella, S., Martinez, A. M., and Pollak, S. D. (2019). Emotional Expressions Reconsidered: Challenges to Inferring Emotion From Human Facial Movements. *Psychological science in the public interest*, 20(1):1–68.

Batliner, A., Neumann, M., Burkhardt, F., Baird, A., Meyer, S., Vu, N. T., and Schuller, B. (2022). Ethical awareness in paralinguistics: A taxonomy of application. *International Journal of Human-Computer Interaction.*

Burkhardt, F., Paeschke, A., Rolfes, M., Sendlmeier, W., and Weiss, B. (2005). A database of german emotional speech. In *9th European Conference on Speech Communication and Technology*, volume 5, pages 1517–1520, 09.

Burkhardt, F., Audibert, N., Malatesta, L., Türk, O., Arslan, L., and Auberge, V. (2006). Emotional prosody - does culture make a difference? In *Proceedings of the International Conference on Speech Prosody.*

Burkhardt, F., Saponja, M., Sessner, J., and Weiss, B. (2019). How should pepper sound - preliminary investigations on robot vocalizations. Peter Birkholz, Simon Stone.

Burkhardt, F., Brückl, M., and Schuller, B. (2021). Age classification: Comparison of human vs machine performance in prompted and spontaneous speech. In Stefan Hillmann, et al., editors, *Studientexte zur Sprachkommunikation: Elektronische Sprachsignalverarbeitung 2021*, pages 35–42. TUD-press, Dresden.

Burkhardt, F., Wagner, J., Wierstorf, H., Eyben, F., and Schuller, B. (2022). Nkululeko: A tool for rapid speaker characteristics detection. In *Proceedings of LREC 2022.*

Burkhardt, F. (2000). *Simulation emotionaler Sprechweise mit Sprachsynthesesystemen.* Shaker.

Burkhardt, F. (2005). Emofilt: The simulation of emotional speech by prosody-transformation. In *9th European Conference on Speech Communication and Technology*.

Cahn, J. (2000). Generation of affect in synthesized speech. *J. Am. Voice I/O Soc.*, 8, 06.

Chen, T. and Guestrin, C. (2016). XGBoost: A scalable tree boosting system. In *Proceedings of the 22nd ACM SIGKDD International Conference on Knowledge Discovery and Data Mining*, KDD '16, pages 785–794, New York, NY, USA. ACM.

Costantini, G., Iaderola, I., Paoloni, A., and Todisco, M. (2014). Emovo corpus: an italian emotional speech database. In *LREC*.

Deng, J., Zhang, Z., Marchi, E., and Schuller, B. W. (2013). Sparse autoencoder-based feature transfer learning for speech emotion recognition. In *ACII*, pages 511–516. IEEE Computer Society.

Deng, J., Zhang, Z., Eyben, F., and Schuller, B. (2014). Autoencoder-based unsupervised domain adaptation for speech emotion recognition. *Signal Processing Letters, IEEE*, 21:1068–1072, 09.

Dutoit, T., Pagel, V., Pierret, N., Bataille, F., and der Vreken, O. (1996). The mbrola project: Towards a set of high-quality speech synthesizers free of use for non-commercial purposes. *Proc. ICSLP'96, Philadelphia*, 3:1393–1396.

Engberg, I. S., Hansen, A. V., Andersen, O., and Dalsgaard, P. (1997). Design, recording and verification of a danish emotional speech database. In *EUROSPEECH*.

Eskimez, S., Dimitriadis, D., Gmyr, R., and Kumanati, K. (2020). Gan-based data generation for speech emotion recognition. In *Proc. Interspeech*, pages 3446–3450, 10.

Eyben, F., Wöllmer, M., and Schuller, B. (2010). opensmile – the munich versatile and fast open-source audio feature extractor. *MM'10 - Proceedings of the ACM Multimedia 2010 International Conference*, pages 1459–1462, 01.

Eyben, F., Scherer, K., Schuller, B., Sundberg, J., Andre, E., Busso, C., Devillers, L., Epps, J., Laukka, P., Narayanan, S., and Truong, K. (2015). The geneva minimalistic acoustic parameter set (gemaps) for voice research and affective computing. *IEEE Transactions on Affective Computing*, 7:1–1, 01.

Feraru, S. M., Schuller, D., and Schuller, B. (2015). Cross-language acoustic emotion recognition: An overview and some tendencies. In *2015 International Conference on Affective Computing and Intelligent Interaction (ACII)*, pages 125–131.

Goldhahn, D., Eckart, T., and Quasthoff, U. (2012). Building large monolingual dictionaries at the leipzig corpora collection: From 100 to 200 languages. In *In Proceedings of the Eight International Conference on Language Resources and Evaluation (LREC'12*.

Kaya, H., Salah, A., Gurgen, F., and Ekenel, H. (2014). Protocol and baseline for experiments on bogazici university turkish emotional speech corpus. In *2014 22nd Signal Processing and Communications Applications Conference, SIU 2014 - Proceedings*, 04.

Latif, S., Rana, R., Khalifa, S., Jurdak, R., Epps, J., and Schuller, B. (2020). Multi-task semi-supervised adversarial autoencoding for speech emotion recognition. *IEEE Transactions on Affective Computing*, PP:1–1, 04.

Livingstone, S. R. and Russo, F. A. (2018). The ryerson audio-visual database of emotional speech and song (RAVDESS): A dynamic, multimodal set of facial and vocal expressions in north american english. *PLOS ONE*, 13(5):e0196391.

Lotfian, R. and Busso, C. (2017). Building naturalistic emotionally balanced speech corpus by retrieving emotional speech from existing podcast recordings. *IEEE Transactions on Affective Computing*, PP:1–1, 08.

Neumann, M. and Vu, T. (2018). Cross-lingual and multilingual speech emotion recognition on english and french. In *2018 IEEE International Conference on Acoustics, Speech and Signal Processing (ICASSP)*, pages 5769–5773, 02.

Powroźnik, P. (2017). Kohonen network as a classifier of polish emotional speech. *ITM Web of Conferences*, 15.

Ringeval, F., Cowie, R., Amiriparian, S., Michaud, A., Schuller, B., Kaya, H., Cummins, N., Çiftçi, E., Valstar, M., Schmitt, M., Lalanne, D., Güleç, H., Salah, A. A., and Pantic, M. (2018). AVEC 2018 Workshop and Challenge: Bipolar disorder and cross-cultural affect recognition. In *AVEC 2018 - Proceedings of the 2018 Audio/Visual Emotion Challenge and Workshop, co-located with MM 2018*.

Scherer, K. R., Banse, R., and Wallbott, H. G. (1999). Emotion Inferences from Vocal Expression Correlate across Languages and Cultures. *ICPhS 99*.

Schröder, M. and Grice, M. (2003). Expressing vocal effort in concatenative synthesis. *Proceedings of the 15th International Conference of Phonetic Sciences*, 09.

Schröder, M. and Trouvain, J. (2003). The german text-to-speech synthesis system mary: A tool for research, development and teaching. *International Journal of Speech Technology*, 6:365–377.

Schuller, B. and Burkhardt, F. (2010). Learning with synthesized speech for automatic emotion recognition. In *2010 IEEE International Conference on Acoustics, Speech and Signal Processing*, pages 5150–5153.

Schuller, B., Zhang, Z., Weninger, F., and Burkhardt, F. (2012). Synthesized speech for model training in cross-corpus recognition of human emotion. *International Journal of Speech Technology*, 15, 09.

Schuller, B., Steidl, S., Batliner, A., Hirschberg, J., Burgoon, J., Baird, A., Elkins, A., Zhang, Y., Coutinho, E., and Evanini, K. (2016). The interspeech 2016 computational paralinguistics challenge: Deception, sincerity and native language. In *Proceedings Interspeech 2016*, pages 2001–2005, 09.

van der Maaten, L. and Hinton, G. (2008). Visualizing data using t-SNE. *Journal of Machine Learning Research*, 9:2579–2605.

Yildirim, S., Bulut, M., Lee, C., Kazemzadeh, A., Lee, S., Narayanan, S., and Busso, C. (2004). An acoustic study of emotions expressed in speech. 10.

Zhou, X., Ling, Z.-H., and King, S. (2020). The blizzard challenge 2020. pages 1–18, 10.

*Proceedings of the 1st Workshop on Dataset Creation for Lower-Resourced Languages (DCLRL) @LREC2022*, pages 10–18
Marseille, 24 June 2022


# Data Sets of Eating Disorders by Categorizing Reddit and Tumblr Posts: A Multilingual Comparative Study Based on Empirical Findings of Texts and Images

**Christina Baskal, Amelie Elisabeth Beutel, Jessika Keberlein, Malte Ollmann, Esra Üresin, Jana Vischinski, Janina Weihe, Linda Achilles, Christa Womser-Hacker**
Department of Information Science and Natural Language Processing
University of Hildesheim, Universitätsplatz 1, 31141 Hildesheim, GER
{baskal, beutel, keberlei, ollmann, ueresin, vischins, weihej, achilles, womser}@uni-hildesheim.de

**Abstract**

Research has shown the potential negative impact of social media usage on body image. Various platforms present numerous medial formats of possibly harmful content related to eating disorders. Different cultural backgrounds, represented, for example, by different languages, are participating in the discussion online. Therefore, this research aims to investigate eating disorder specific content in a multilingual and multimedia environment. We want to contribute to establishing a common ground for further automated approaches. Our first objective is to combine the two media formats, text and image, by classifying the posts from one social media platform (Reddit) and continuing the categorization in the second (Tumblr). Our second objective is the analysis of multilingualism. We worked qualitatively in an iterative valid categorization process, followed by a comparison of the portrayal of eating disorders on both platforms. Our final data sets contained 960 Reddit and 2 081 Tumblr posts. Our analysis revealed that Reddit users predominantly exchange content regarding disease and eating behaviour, while on Tumblr, the focus is on the portrayal of oneself and one's body.

**Keywords:** Tumblr, Reddit, data set, social media analysis, content analysis, multilinguality, eating disorders, multimedia, language resource

## 1. Introduction

Eating disorders (ED) are a major health issue affecting many adolescents and young adults. The National Eating Disorder Association (NEDA), for instance, reported that approximately 20 million women and 10 million men in America will suffer from an eating disorder at some point in their lives (NEDA, 2021). A review of the prevalence and incidence of eating disorders (Hoek and van Hoeken, 2003) also reveals that only one out of three people in the general population with stringent diagnostic criteria receives treatment. Some sufferers declare their illness to be a legitimate, alternative lifestyle choice (Hoek and van Hoeken, 2003; Fox et al., 2005; Norris et al., 2006).
Therefore, the main purpose of this research is to explore the challenges that multimedia and multilingual social media texts and images pose for categorization and automated processing. We pursue the goal of extracting texts and images from two social media platforms Reddit[1] (text in English) and Tumblr[2] (text and image in German, English, Russian and Turkish). While the most diverse age groups from various countries increasingly spend time on social networks, it simultaneously gains interest to investigate factors such as grammar structure, content and the combination of text and image. Hence, we provided two data sets, including the media formats, text and image, that form a basis for automatic analyses. The first data set is based on the eRisk data from 2018[3], consists of Reddit posts concerning ED. We further extended this data by means of a categorization procedure and referred to it as Reddit data set (RDS). The second, the Tumblr data set (TDS), was crafted by us by collecting images and their descriptions from Tumblr[4] We contribute to the ongoing research by enriching both data sets with our categorization, respectively.
The present study will (1) compare the topics discussed in ED communities of the two Social Media platforms, Reddit and Tumblr, by classifying the posts based on a qualitative content analysis approach and (2) investigate the differences of the four languages that are subject to our analyses.

## 2. Related Work

Past research has shown the impact of media consumption (magazines and TV) on disordered eating (Grabe et al., 2008). Also the influence of social media engagement on dysfunctional eating habits was investigated. One study found that already a short Facebook use of 20 minutes is associated with body weight and shape concerns in their study participants (Mabe et al., 2014). Another shows that Internet exposure correlates signif-

[1] Website of the social network Reddit: https://www.reddit.com/

[2] Website of the social network Tumblr: https://www.tumblr.com/

[3] Access to the research collection can be granted by following the instruction found on the website https://tec.citius.usc.es/ir/code/eRisk.html

[4] For access to the TDS, please contact the authors.

icantly with the internalisation of beauty ideals, body surveillance, and the drive for thinness (Tiggemann and Slater, 2013).
Automatic approaches of social media text analyses were used to measure the mental illness severity of anorectic internet users (Chancellor et al., 2016a) or to examine lexical variations of hashtags that derived after the banning of specific pro eating disorder (pro-ED) tags (Chancellor et al., 2016c). Other researchers have examined YouTube comments in different ED communities (pro-ED and the opposing anti-pro-ED community) based on their sentiments (Oksanen et al., 2015), Twitter tweets and how ED symptoms are discussed there (Cavazos-Rehg et al., 2019) and Reddit ED-community differences (Fettach and Benhiba, 2019).
Reddit is also in the focus of the eRisk Lab (early Risk Detection on the Internet)[5] that is held in conjunction with the CLEF Initiative (Conference and Labs of the Evaluation Forum)[6]. The main objective of eRisk is to provide a forum for the evaluation methodologies, performance metrics, and building of test collections concerning issues of health and safety on the internet (Losada et al., 2019). For that purpose, the organisers arranged shared tasks and provide associated data sets. In 2018 and 2019, the early detection of anorexia nervosa by sequentially processing Reddit posts was part of the challenge. The data set of 2018 was used in this paper also and is further described in section 3.1. Another study utilized likewise the anorexia data set of eRisk 2019 to analyse topical trends in anorectic Reddit users (Masood et al., 2020). The lab also puts emphasis on other mental disorders such as self-harm and depression, which patients of eating disorders are considered to be engaging with also (Hudson et al., 2007; Turner et al., 2015; Wang et al., 2017). Our institute also researched the early signs of self-harm (Achilles et al., 2020) and the severity of depression (Bandyopadhyay et al., 2019) of Reddit users in the past using the eRisk data sets.
Anorexia and its depiction on Tumblr was also the target of research in the past (Choudhury, 2015; Wick and Harriger, 2018). Other work studied the differences in the communication about it on Twitter and Tumblr (Branley and Covey, 2017) and more research on anorexia related imagery showed that pictures showing body parts (thin thighs/legs, flat stomachs, protruding hip bones, ribs or collar bones) are most common in the online discussions (Cavazos-Rehg et al., 2019). Another image-based study collected Instagram pictures and qualitatively classified them (Ging and Garvey, 2018). More work on differentiating the imagery of ED-content, represented by the hashtags *thinspiration* and *bonespiration* from the concept of *fitspiration* was done by Talbot and colleagues (Talbot et al., 2017).

[5]Website of the eRisk Lab: https://erisk.irlab.org/

[6]Website of the CLEF initiative: http://www.clef-initiative.eu/

All studies presented here were investigating either linguistic phenomena in the English language, or were retrieving ED-related imagery by utilizing English hashtags.

## 3. Methodological Approach

Figure 1 represents our workflow. Each individual project step is discussed in more detail in the following sections.

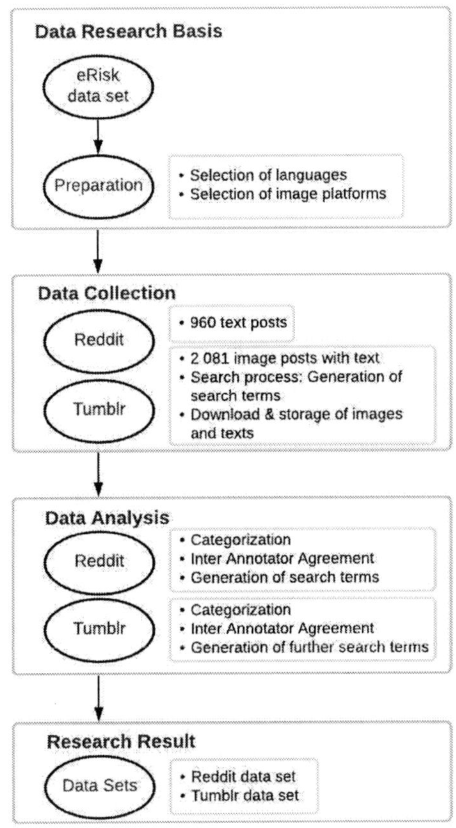


Figure 1: The four stages of our methodological approach, with a focus on qualitative data categorization

### 3.1. Data Research Basis

Our starting point was the eRisk data set[7], that we defined as the baseline for our methodological approach (see Fig. 1). The data collection process is further described in the work of Losada and Crestani (Losada and Crestani, 2016). The data set was published as part of the CLEF eRisk workshop 2018 (Losada et al., 2018). A distinction is made between training and test data.

[7]Information on the eRisk data collection of 2018 and how to access it can be found here: https://tec.citius.usc.es/ir/code/eRisk.html

We referred solely to the training files. They were subdivided into positive and negative examples. In the context of our research, we worked exclusively with the positive examples, i.e., Reddit posts that explicitly came from users diagnosed with anorexia. Of the total of 152 participants, who were designated as subjects and anonymized by means of a subjectID, 20 people suffered from anorexia. We only analysed the posts of 18 since our review showed that two of them did not write about anorectic content. The Reddit posts were XML files presented in the form of 10 chunks. Each chunk consisted of 20 XML files, which summed up a total of 200 XML files. Furthermore, a chunk provides a chronological sequence: Therefore, chunk 1 contains posts that are further away in time than, for example, chunk 10. For our research, we went through all the posts manually.

### Preparation

We selected four languages to investigate differences in the representation of ED given the images, image descriptions or hashtags. The literature review revealed that English is discussed predominantly. However, Russian, Turkish, and German are under-represented in the scientific research so far. We decided to use German, English, Russian and Turkish to examine the ED discourse on social media platforms. To accomplish our research aim, we defined four criteria for selecting an appropriate social media portal: 1) focus on mutual exchange of content, 2) multilingual searches that display results, 3) visibility of sensitive content and 4) download option of images and meta data. Tumblr thus covered all the criteria we previously decided on.

## 3.2. Data Collection & Data Analysis

First, we started the categorization by looking into the eRisk data set to gain an insight into the architecture of the data set. We defined the goal of the categorization at the beginning in the form of a list of categories that can describe the content of the Reddit posts. Then, we determined to use both main and sub-categories. Each post was assigned one or more main categories and an arbitrary number of matching sub-categories. The sub-categories serve to define the main categories and describe the context of the posts in more detail. The creation of the category list was an iterative process inspired by the taxonomy generation method of Nickerson et al. (2013). Nickerson et al. (2013) accentuate the importance to record end criteria when working iteratively. We defined both subjective and objective end criteria for our approach at the outset. The objective end criterion was that every Reddit post could be classified with at least one main category. For the subjective one, we determined that the categorization must be useful and able to describe the Reddit posts. We all worked together on the first chunk of Reddit posts in the first iteration and thus generated an initial list of main and sub-categories. Then we divided the remaining chunks and worked independently, meeting periodically to discuss new category suggestions. All in all, 6 492 posts were dropped during this process due to the fact that those contained content unrelated to our research, for instance, discussions about online games. 960 posts were reviewed and classified qualitatively by the group.

The **Inter Annotator Agreement (IAA)**, we performed to ensure an objective categorization, shows that we achieved a Fleiss' Kappa values of 0.86 for the Reddit posts and 0.83 for the Tumblr posts. Referring to Table 1, both values show near-perfect agreement between the annotators at over 80% (Landis and Koch, 1977). Each annotator independently assigned categories for the first 10% of the RDS and TDS, while only one main category could be assigned to each post.

| Fleiss' Kappa | Interpretation |
|---|---|
| <0.00 | Poor agreement |
| 0.00 to 0.20 | Slight agreement |
| 0.21 to 0.40 | Fair agreement |
| 0.41 to 0.60 | Moderate agreement |
| 0.61 to 0.80 | Substantial agreement |
| 0.81 to 1.00 | Almost perfect |

Table 1: Interpretation of Fleiss' Kappa value thresholds

While we categorized the Reddit posts, we also extracted search terms for the later usage on Tumblr. Those would come from prominent words or topics which had to be related to ED and written in the posts. Besides, we found some ED-specific names of brands and new words related to the ED-culture, for instance, *thinspo*. This finding also overlaps with the study results presented in our literature review. *Thinspiration*, of which thinspo is the abbreviation, was the subject of study in different research settings (Wick and Harriger, 2018; Ging and Garvey, 2018; Talbot et al., 2017). While we initially generated those individually, we would draft the first list later. In this process, duplicates and search terms that were too broad would be deleted. Meanwhile, all of them were translated into the previously selected languages by the native speakers in our team. Furthermore, we collected exceptional ED-specific search terms because they could not be translated. Those were words used by the ED community and abbreviations we found.

After generating various search items based on the Reddit posts, we started the first search process on Tumblr to check which terms could be considered further. We were looking specifically for posts with (moving) images that can be saved or an image in the form of text, not a text-only post, which correlated with the Reddit categories. During the initial search, we generated more items by looking at the hashtags and texts under the posts. At the same time, we suspected that these new words were relevant because we frequently saw them during our Tumblr searches. After this process, we found 56 new search items, 26 of which were

| Language | Search Terms |
|---|---|
| English | anorexia relapse, restriction |
| ED-specific | Ana, an0rex1a |
| Russian | голод, анорексичка |
| German | Abführmittel, fasten |
| Turkish | yeme bozukluğu |

Table 2: Example search terms out of the final 127

| Language | Search Terms % | Posts % |
|---|---|---|
| English | 57 (44.9%) | 902 (43.3%) |
| ED-specific | 33 (26%) | 639 (30.7%) |
| Russian | 21 (16.5%) | 350 (16.8%) |
| German | 15 (11.8%) | 182 (8.7%) |
| Turkish | 1 (0.8%) | 8 (0.4%) |
| **Total** | 127 (100%) | 2 081 (100%) |

Table 3: Absolute numbers and probability distribution of final search terms per language

new ED-specific terms.

Following the initial search process on Tumblr, we colour-coded the words into relevant, irrelevant, and no hits to filter out the relevant search terms.

Table 2 shows example search terms of our final list after the completion of the above-mentioned processing steps.

We decided to look at the first 20 relevant image posts per relevant term during the second search process.

We downloaded these images and assigned them an appropriate ID. Additionally, we extracted descriptive metadata, such as captions and hashtags. Since a post could contain multiple images, the maximum number of images was therefore not 20 but could be exceeded. If a post contained more than one image, we marked that in the ID by simply extending it by a new number for the sub-post. Every item with less than three posts was irrelevant and deleted. Furthermore, we noticed that previously relevant ones were no longer relevant because they were textual. According to our criteria, we had to deliberately exclude such contributions, even if they would have been relevant in terms of content. The final composition of the successful ones can be taken from Table 3.

### 3.3. Research Result

In the following, we present the finalized categorization of both data sets.

#### Reddit Data Set

In this part we will go into more detail on how we proceeded analytically. For a complete list of all the possible main and sub-categories, please refer to Figure 2. According to the user agreement with the eRisk organizers, it is not permitted to show example posts of the RDS. Therefore, we describe here our general approach to analyze the posts. For instance, if a user referred to food and mealtime, this post would be categorized as eating behaviour (as represented in Figure 2 with the grey highlighted row) because its main content revolves around what and when to eat. Furthermore, the words *meal plan* and *calories* are mentioned explicitly (likewise highlighted in the white boxes). These are indicators for the respective sub-categories. If a poster writes about their wish to get better and sustain a healthier lifestyle, it implies the main category of disease and the sub-category desire for recovery. A combination of several main and sub-categories is also possible. If a user referred to several sports and an exercise plan in their post, we would classify it with the main category urge to exercise and the corresponding sub-categories question about physiology and sports activities.

#### Tumblr Data Set

As already mentioned, it is impossible to construct a complete data set of Tumblr posts, meaning the total period of ED-related writings starting from the beginning of Tumblr itself. In this case, an opportunistic selection was chosen. This means that the amount of content determines data availability. It has been noted that in a couple of search terms, the same posts reoccurred after the approximate number of 20 posts. Therefore, we decided to focus on this specific amount to rightfully manage an appropriate number of posts for the random sample and provide no duplicate posts within a search term. Furthermore, it is important to define the amount of selection specifically. In this part, we consolidated our whole retrieved Tumblr data into one data set, namely TDS. Like we did for the Reddit posts, we created a table for the writings we retrieved from Tumblr. The table contains multiple columns, each concentrated explicitly on a specific topic. The first column was generated to retrieve and organize our search terms more effectively, which were already explained in the previous section 3.2.

The next column showed the Reddit main categories that were explained in the previous section 3.3.

In the following column we specified the types of the Tumblr images. Prior to that, we have given some definitions for some types to ensure an unanimous understanding within the team. Our findings on Tumblr showed that the following eight categories occurred the most: *drawing*, *food*, *person*, *meme*, *medication*, *fashion*, *text* and also allowing the option *other* if none of the other types were suitable.

Sometimes the pictures on their own were not identifiable and therefore required some of the metadata like the caption and hashtags for a better understanding. Consequently, we concluded that creating separate columns was necessary.

One of these columns is regarding the multilingualism of the posts. Here, we marked if the hashtags and/or the caption is written in more than one language. In Fig. 5, we marked that there is no multilingual text/hashtags through 'no' and coded the identified language English as '2'.

| main category | 1) urge to exercise | 2) eating behaviour | 3) state of anxiety | 4) perception of body and weight | 5) disease | 6) community |
|---|---|---|---|---|---|---|
| sub-category | a) question about physiology | a) call for help | a) call for help | a) comparison with other people | a) biographical content | a) comparison within the community |
| | b) sport activities | b) calories | b) fear of non-self-control | b) external perception | b) daily routine | b) negative support |
| | | c) fasting | c) fear of rejection/bad feedback | c) inspiration | c) desire for recovery | c) negative tips |
| | | d) loss of control | d) fear of relapse | d) own body perception | d) diagnosis | d) positive support |
| | | e) meal plan | e) fear that acquaintances will find out | e) positive feedback to own looks/body | e) emotionality | e) positive tips |
| | | f) recipe | f) question about physiology/fear of loss of control | f) revulsion | f) fear of recovery | |
| | | g) rejection of specific products | | g) weight gain/loss/data | g) medication | |
| | | h) supporting products | | | h) mental illness | |
| | | i) time of the meal | | | i) relapse | |
| | | | | | j) side effects of disease | |
| | | | | | k) therapy | |

Figure 2: Complete list of main and sub-categories of the RDS and TDS

| search term | mapping of the main category | picture classification | multilingual text/hashtags | languages | text | hashtags |
|---|---|---|---|---|---|---|
| en_body_check_09 | perception of body and weight | person | no | 2 | My body checks are so different | #bodycheck#thinspo#thinspiration#my photo#skinny#slim#skinny girl |
| en_body_check_10 | perception of body and weight | person | no | 2 | I don't like how my body looks. | #ana#pro ana#anorexia#not pro just for myself#ana tips#ana diary |
| en_body_check_11 | perception of body and weight | person | no | 2 | My body check! | #anamiia#anamia#anamiiia#anarexia#anarexix |

Figure 3: An excerpt from the Tumblr data set using the search term "body check" and the main category "perception of body and weight" as an example

To get an idea of the TDS and to retrace our analysis and categorization process, we prepared a graphic with six sample images for each main category (see Fig. 5). We deliberately chose examples for this paper that do not contain inappropriate images of body parts such as thin legs or collar bones which may be disturbing for the readers, or pictures that violate the anonymity of the users.

## 4. Findings and Discussion

With our work, we contribute to the scientific community by combining a Tumblr and Reddit data set to examine how eating disorders are discussed and how the use of multilingualism is distributed. By applying a common category list, we could compare both data sets. The posts can be analysed in three ways: one and only one term was stated (*single*), the examined term and additionally, one or several terms were stated (*multiple*) and several terms are combined (*combination*).

One of the main findings is that the categories perception of body and weight, eating behaviour and disease are the most frequent ones for both platforms. The finding that the image category person was found the most in both single and multiple distribution supports the idea that Tumblr is a photo-based platform. Here, both self-expression, as well as the portrayal of the body, are at the centre of users. Writing about one's behaviour

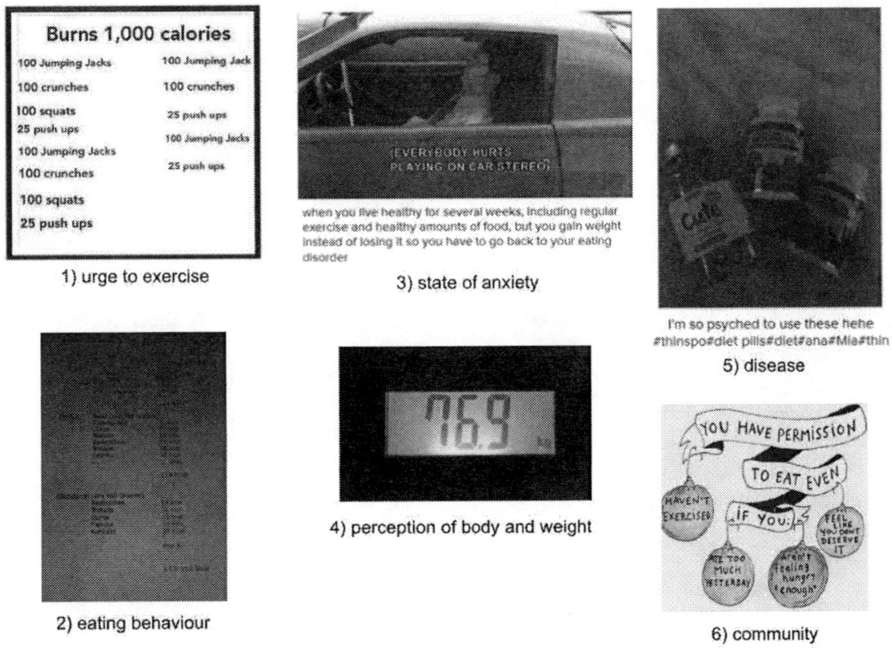


Figure 4: Example images from the Tumblr data set, sorted by different main categories. 1) Shows a workout plan, 2) a meal plan including calories, 3) a meme on ED, 4) the display of a scale, 5) a set of diet pill bottles, 6) an encouraging community post against ED

is probably easier than communicating the same content via image and a short description with hashtags, which reasons that Reddit as a text-based social media platform mainly discusses topics such as disease and eating behaviour. As Cavazos-Rehg et al. (2019) discussed in their paper, the categories body shape, eating concerns and weight concerns appeared in descending order. We cannot compare these categories one-to-one with our category list, as we combined posts regarding body shape and weight concern in the category perception of body and weight. Furthermore, just as Cavazos-Rehg et al. (2019) and Wick and Harriger (2018), we also found that the search term *thinspiration* led to images of body parts such as thin legs and stomachs as well as before-after images. Compared to the image-based study conducted by Ging and Garvey (2018), we found similar categories but distinguished them differently. For instance, our main category disease includes the sub-category mental illness, which contains depression, self-harm and suicide, which all come up in their study. Further, their categories pro-recovery and selfie pictures are also represented in our study with variable names. In contrast to their categorization, we subdivided the images categories in a more incremental approach relevant to the content displayed.

The discussion of Mental Illness Severity topics on both social media platforms focuses on the self-portrayal, eating behaviour and disease of a user. These findings overlap with Chancellor et al. (2016a): Here, one of the three main markers is excessive weight control. Specifically, on Tumblr, we found that (pro-)ED-specific hashtags were applied. This supports Chancellor et al. (2016c) and Chancellor et al. (2016b) findings. Prior to the Tumblr data extraction, the team shifted awareness to the sensitive content that is shared on the social media platform. Whenever a team member felt overwhelmed, it was shared and another team member took over going through the texts and images.

The language distribution can only be considered on Tumblr as the Reddit posts were all in English. Over 85% of all Tumblr posts were monolingual. The multiple distribution of languages indicates that the most commonly used language was English, followed by Russian, German, other languages and Turkish in descending order. German and English was the most common language combination, followed by English and Russian. That indicates that English functions as a lingua franca to reach a large audience, either solely or in combination with other stated languages.

The language distribution of successful search terms also shows that English with 41% was the language with the most search results. However, as the classification of ED-specific search terms is not an official language but rather a set of ED-specific vocabulary, it is not surprising that they led to the second most oc-

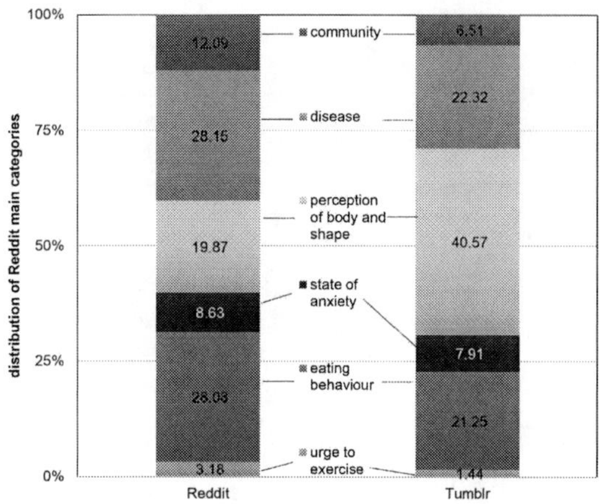


Figure 5: Comparison of Reddit main categories on Reddit and Tumblr in percentage

| Categories | EN | ED | RU | DE | TR |
|---|---|---|---|---|---|
| no Reddit main Category | 11 (1.5%) | 24 (4.2%) | 0 (0%) | 6 (4%) | 0 (0%) |
| urge to exercise | 9 (1.2%) | 2 (0.3%) | 0 (0%) | 2 (0.3%) | 0 (0%) |
| eating behavior | 184 (25.4%) | 110 (19.4%) | 37 (13.9%) | 18 (11.9%) | 0 (0%) |
| state of anxiety | 12 (1.7%) | 31 (5.5%) | 14 (5.2%) | 3 (2%) | 0 (0%) |
| perception of body & weight | 323 (44.6%) | 310 (54.6%) | 167 (62.8%) | 69 (45.7%) | 3 (100%) |
| disease | 158 (21.9%) | 78 (13.7%) | 39 (14.7%) | 46 (30.5%) | 0 (0%) |
| community | 27 (3.7%) | 13 (2.3) | 9 (3.4%) | 7 (4.6%) | 0 (0%) |
| **Total** | 724 (100%) | 568 (100%) | 266 (100%) | 151 (100%) | 3 (100%) |

Table 4: Category distribution for the total amount and percentage of languages of posts on Tumblr

curred results with 35%.

The category distribution of each language (see Table 4) shows that perception of body and weight was the most discussed topic in all languages indicating that this is a dominant subject regarding ED. For English and ED-specific terms, eating behaviour was the second most commonly used category, while for Russian and German posts, the most prevailing category was disease.

We observed that ED-specific terms were frequently combined with the given languages German, English, Russian, Turkish and/or other languages. For instance, one of the 33 ED-specific terms is thinspiration and often occurs in combination with our selected languages. These combinations were visible either in the post description, in hashtags and/or, in some cases, as text on an image. However, we did not quantitatively analyse the distribution of ED-specific terms and other languages. That would be interesting research to resume on our current findings.

## 5. Limitations and Future Directions

As the data validation showed, the respective languages' results were not balanced, as Turkish had only one relevant search term. Despite the lack of Turkish-language data, it was possible to conclude that in the ED context on Tumblr, English hashtags are predominantly used by users speaking other languages as well. This can be justified by the fact that users can better express their sense of belonging in this particular community this way, and users may find a larger community with common interests. Regarding our small Turkish data set, we found a study from Bulut and Doğan (2017) showing that Tumblr is one of the more unpopular social media networking sites in Turkey. This is in accordance to a statistic from Clement (2022) published in March 2022, which shows, network-traffic from Turkey to Tumblr.com being almost non-existent. Further research can follow up on our study by considering additional languages and other image platforms. In addition, more Reddit and Tumblr posts could be analyzed to improve the data sets. The data collection can be used for machine processing in further steps to use automatic methods. Furthermore, our collected data can be trained for image recognition: The system learns the defined categories and can match them with the hashtags and images used. This could be helpful for the early detection of eating disorders. Moreover, the texts can be examined linguistically. For instance, the distribution of ED-specific terms in posts could be examined regarding the language combination of monolingual and/or multilingual posts. The special terms as a language-independent construct can be further explored in more in-depth research.

## 6. Ethical Considerations

The Tumblr posts used in this study were publicly available. The names used by blog authors are fictional. However, in the data set the names were removed and only images, texts and hashtags of the posts were kept. The data set is saved on university servers behind password protection. Quotes have been slightly altered to further protect the individuals who have written these social media contributions. Therefore, a jurisdiction of our university's Ethics Commission is not required for this study.

## 7. References

Achilles, L., Kisselew, M., Schäfer, J., and Kölle, R. (2020). Using Surface and Semantic Features for Detecting Early Signs of Self-Harm in Social Media Postings. In Linda Cappellato, et al., editors, *Working Notes of CLEF 2020 - Conference and Labs of the Evaluation Forum, Thessaloniki, Greece, September 22-25, 2020*, volume 2696 of *CEUR Workshop Proceedings*. CEUR-WS.org.

Bandyopadhyay, A., Achilles, L., Mandl, T., Mitra, M., and Saha, S. K. (2019). Identification of Depression Severity for Users of Online Platforms. In Robert Jäschke et al., editors, *Proceedings of the Conference on "Lernen, Wissen, Daten, Analysen", Berlin, Germany, September 30 - October 2, 2019*, volume 2454 of *CEUR Workshop Proceedings*, pages 331–342. CEUR-WS.org.

Branley, D. B. and Covey, J. (2017). Pro-ana versus pro-recovery: A content analytic comparison of social media users' communication about eating disorders on Twitter and Tumblr. *Frontiers in Psychology*, 8:1356.

Bulut, Z. A. and Doğan, O. (2017). The abcd typology: Profile and motivations of turkish social network sites users. *Computers in Human Behavior*, 67:73–83.

Cavazos-Rehg, P. A., Krauss, M. J., Costello, S. J., Kaiser, N., Cahn, E. S., Fitzsimmons-Craft, E. E., and Wilfley, D. E. (2019). "I just want to be skinny.": A content analysis of tweets expressing eating disorder symptoms. *PloS one*, 14(1):e0207506.

Chancellor, S., Lin, Z., Goodman, E. L., Zerwas, S., and Choudhury, M. D. (2016a). Quantifying and Predicting Mental Illness Severity in Online Pro-Eating Disorder Communities. In Darren Gergle, et al., editors, *Proceedings of the 19th ACM Conference on Computer-Supported Cooperative Work & Social Computing, CSCW 2016, San Francisco, CA, USA, February 27 - March 2, 2016*, pages 1169–1182. ACM.

Chancellor, S., Lin, Z. J., and Choudhury, M. D. (2016b). "This Post Will Just Get Taken Down": Characterizing Removed Pro-Eating Disorder Social Media Content. In Jofish Kaye, et al., editors, *Proceedings of the 2016 CHI Conference on Human Factors in Computing Systems, San Jose, CA, USA, May 7-12, 2016*, pages 1157–1162. ACM.

Chancellor, S., Pater, J. A., Clear, T. A., Gilbert, E., and Choudhury, M. D. (2016c). #thyghgapp: Instagram Content Moderation and Lexical Variation in Pro-Eating Disorder Communities. In Darren Gergle, et al., editors, *Proceedings of the 19th ACM Conference on Computer-Supported Cooperative Work & Social Computing, CSCW 2016, San Francisco, CA, USA, February 27 - March 2, 2016*, pages 1199–1211. ACM.

Choudhury, M. D. (2015). Anorexia on Tumblr: A Characterization Study. In Patty Kostkova et al., editors, *Proceedings of the 5th International Conference on Digital Health 2015, Florence, Italy, May 18-20, 2015*, pages 43–50. ACM.

Clement, J. (2022). May.

Fettach, Y. and Benhiba, L. (2019). Pro-Eating Disorders and Pro-Recovery Communities on Reddit: Text and Network Comparative Analyses. In *Proceedings of the 21st International Conference on Information Integration and Web-based Applications & Services, iiWAS 2019, Munich, Germany, December 2-4, 2019*, pages 277–286. ACM.

Fox, N., Ward, K., and O'rourke, A. (2005). Pro-anorexia, Weight-loss Drugs and the Internet: an 'Anti-recovery' Explanatory Model of Anorexia. *Sociology of health & illness*, 27(7):944–971.

Ging, D. and Garvey, S. (2018). 'Written in these scars are the stories I can't explain': A Content Analysis of Pro-ana and Thinspiration Image Sharing on Instagram. *New Media Soc.*, 20(3):1181–1200.

Grabe, S., Ward, L. M., and Hyde, J. S. (2008). The Role of the Media in Body Image Concerns among Women: A meta-analysis of Experimental and Correlational Studies. *Psychological Bulletin*, 134(3):460.

Hoek, H. W. and van Hoeken, D. (2003). Review of the Prevalence and Incidence of Eating Disorders. *The International Journal of Eating Disorders*, 34:838–396.

Hudson, J. I., Hiripi, E., Pope Jr, H. G., and Kessler, R. C. (2007). The Prevalence and Correlates of Eating Disorders in the National Comorbidity Survey Replication. *Biological psychiatry*, 61(3):348–358.

Landis, J. and Koch, G. (1977). The Measurement of Observer Agreement for Categorical Data. *Biometrics*, 33(1):159–174.

Losada, D. E. and Crestani, F. (2016). A Test Collection for Research on Depression and Language Use. In *International Conference of the Cross-Language Evaluation Forum for European Languages*, pages 28–39. Springer.

Losada, D. E., Crestani, F., and Parapar, J. (2018). Overview of eRisk: Early Risk Prediction on the Internet. In Patrice Bellot, et al., editors, *Experimental IR Meets Multilinguality, Multimodality, and Interaction - 9th International Conference of the CLEF Association, CLEF 2018, Avignon, France, September 10-14, 2018, Proceedings*, volume 11018 of *Lecture Notes in Computer Science*, pages 343–361. Springer.

Losada, D. E., Crestani, F., and Parapar, J. (2019). Overview of eRisk 2019 Early Risk Prediction on the Internet. In *International Conference of the Cross-Language Evaluation Forum for European Languages*, pages 340–357. Springer.

Mabe, A. G., Forney, K. J., and Keel, P. K. (2014). Do you "like" my photo? Facebook use maintains eating disorder risk. *International Journal of Eating Disorders*, 47(5):516–523.

Masood, R., Hu, M., Fabregat, H., Aker, A., and Fuhr, N. (2020). Anorexia Topical Trends in Self-declared Reddit Users. In Iván Cantador, et al., editors, *Proceedings of the First Joint Conference of the Information Retrieval Communities in Europe (CIRCLE 2020), Samatan, Gers, France, July 6-9, 2020*, volume 2621 of *CEUR Workshop Proceedings*. CEUR-WS.org.

NEDA. (2021). What Are Eating Disorders? Available online at: https://www.nationaleatingdisorders.org/what-are-eating-disorders (last retrieved: 17.08.2021).

Nickerson, R. C., Varshney, U., and Muntermann, J. (2013). A Method for Taxonomy Development and its Application in Information Systems. *European Journal of Information Systems*, 22:336–359.

Norris, M. L., Boydell, K. M., Pinhas, L., and Katzman, D. K. (2006). Ana and the Internet: A Review of Pro-anorexia Websites. *International Journal of Eating Disorders*, 39(6):443–447.

Oksanen, A., Garcia, D., Sirola, A., Näsi, M., Kaakinen, M., Keipi, T., and Räsänen, P. (2015). Pro-Anorexia and Anti-Pro-Anorexia Videos on YouTube: Sentiment Analysis of User Responses . *Journal of Medical Internet Research*, 17(11):e256.

Talbot, C. V., Gavin, J., Van Steen, T., and Morey, Y. (2017). A Content Analysis of Thinspiration, Fitspiration, and Bonespiration Imagery on Social Media. *Journal of eating disorders*, 5(1):1–8.

Tiggemann, M. and Slater, A. (2013). NetGirls: The Internet, Facebook, and Body Image concern in adolescent girls. *International Journal of Eating Disorders*, 46(6):630–633.

Turner, B. J., Yiu, A., Layden, B. K., Claes, L., Zaitsoff, S., and Chapman, A. L. (2015). Temporal Associations Between Disordered Eating and Nonsuicidal Self-injury: Examining Symptom Overlap Over 1 Year. *Behavior Therapy*, 46(1):125–138.

Wang, Y., Tang, J., Li, J., Li, B., Wan, Y., Mellina, C., O'Hare, N., and Chang, Y. (2017). Understanding and Discovering Deliberate Self-harm Content in Social Media. In Rick Barrett, et al., editors, *Proceedings of the 26th International Conference on World Wide Web, WWW 2017, Perth, Australia, April 3-7, 2017*, pages 93–102. ACM.

Wick, M. R. and Harriger, J. A. (2018). A Content Analysis of Thinspiration Images and Text Posts on Tumblr. *Body Image*, 24:13–16.

*Proceedings of the 1st Workshop on Dataset Creation for Lower-Resourced Languages (DCLRL) @LREC2022*, pages 19–26
Marseille, 24 June 2022


# Construction and Validation of a Japanese Honorific Corpus Based on Systemic Functional Linguistics

**Muxuan Liu, Ichiro Kobayashi**
Ochanomizu University
{liu.muxuan, koba}@is.ocha.ac.jp

**Abstract**

In Japanese, there are different expressions used in speech depending on the speaker's and listener's social status, called honorifics. Unlike other languages, Japanese has many types of honorific expressions, and it is vital for machine translation and dialogue systems to handle the differences in meaning correctly. However, there is still no corpus that deals with honorific expressions based on social status. In this study, we developed an honorific corpus (KeiCO corpus) that includes social status information based on Systemic Functional Linguistics, which expresses language use in situations from the social group's values and common understanding. As a general-purpose language resource, it filled in the Japanese honorific blanks. We expect the KeiCO corpus could be helpful for various tasks, such as improving the accuracy of machine translation, automatic evaluation, correction of Japanese composition and style transformation. We also verified the accuracy of our corpus by a BERT-based classification task. We release our corpus KeiCO for further research: `https://github.com/Liumx2020/KeiCO-corpus/blob/main/keico_corpus.csv`.

**Keywords:** Japanese corpus, honorific level, systemic functional linguistics

## 1. Introduction

Japanese honorific or Keigo (敬語) is an expression of respect used in Japanese to indicate social rank, intimacy and other relationships among the speaker, the listener and the person mentioned in the conversation.(Aapakallio, 2021)

In many social situations in Japan, honorifics are necessary to express appropriate social status relationships and politeness. Japanese honorifics are generally divided into three categories: respectful (sonkeigo, 尊敬語), humble (kenjogo, 謙譲語), polite (teineigo, 丁寧語). In addition, depending on the content of the conversation and the listener, the speaker may use honorific prefixes, verb morphing, which forms two particular types of honorific: word beautification (bikago, 美化語), and courteous language (teichogo, 丁重語).

However, there is no corpus that contains detailed information on the language used by social groups, such as the situation of language use, social role relationships among interlocutors, and means of interaction. Therefore, it is not easy to construct a machine learning model that takes social factors into account and uses appropriate honorifics.

In this study, we attempt to construct and validate a Japanese honorific corpus (**KeiCO corpus**) which contains more detailed information on social factors based on systemic functional linguistics, which analyzes language from the viewpoint of language use in social groups. We will also make the constructed KeiCO corpus available as a language resource.

Our work has the following contributions.

- We contributed a corpus of 10,007 Japanese sentences. It is the first corpus about honorific sentences. The corpus is based on systemic functional linguistics and contains detailed information on the honorific level, the social relationship between the speaker and the listener, and conversational situations or topics. They filled in the honorific blanks of machine translation, dialogue system, and semantic analysis.
- On the base of our corpus, we took another step on analysis and we got some characteristics of honorific sentences. Through these characteristics, we can help people to better understand honorific sentences under natural circumstances.

## 2. Related Work

Because politeness is usually regarded as a style, the level of honorifics in Japanese can be thought of as several different politeness styles.

Recently, there is much research using machine learning to deal with the politeness of sentences. For example, Resmi and Naseer (2019) created a politeness classifier to classify responses as polite, rude or neutral. Niu and Bansal (2018a) proposed three weakly supervised models that could generate different polite (or rude) conversational responses in the absence of parallel data.

In addition, a lot of controllable natural language generation (NLG) research develop generation methods that incorporate various style transformations, such as length, politeness, perspective, descriptiveness, emotion, and so on (Tsai et al., 2021; Liu et al., 2022). Tsai et al. (2021) propose schema-guided NLG focusing on semantic stylistic control, and showed that disentangling context generation and stylistic variations is more effective at achieving semantic correctness and style accuracy. Liu et al. (2022) propose an Edit-Invariant Sequence Loss (EISL), which computes the matching loss

of a target $n$-gram with all $n$-grams in the generated sequence, and shows the usefulness of EISL applying it to style transferred NLG.
In the task of polite style transformation for English, Madaan et al. (2020) introduce a new task of politeness transfer which involves converting non-polite sentences to polite sentences while preserving the meaning. They also provide a dataset of more than 1.39 million instances from Enron corpus following the same pre-processing by Shetty and Adibi (Klimt and Yang, 2004) , and assign politeness scores to those sentences by using a politeness classifier (Niu and Bansal, 2018b). There are some existing corpora of English that use manual annotation of the politeness and formality of utterances. For example, Rao and Tetreault (2018) has been studied to classify sentences into six levels of formality; and Danescu-Niculescu-Mizil et al. (2013) requires the annotator to indicate how polite she or he considers the request to be using a slider from "very impolite" to "very polite", normalized by a standard Z-score to obtain a definite value. However, there has been no work related to assigning ranks to Japanese honorifics and paraphrasing between the ranks. This is due to two reasons: (1) no corpus exists to support such work, and (2) existing NLP models are not mature enough in their treatment of honorifics. For example, Feely et al. (2019) classifies Japanese sentences into one of three levels of informal, polite or formal speech in parallel texts.

They used the NMT model to learn the difference in the degree of formality in Japanese by identifying honorifics in Japanese in parallel training data and by labelling the source language with additional features. This is a way to control the level of formality of Japanese output in English to Japanese Neural Machine Translation (NMT). However, by simply classifying sentences as informal, polite or formal speech, important linguistic information such as respectful speech and modest speech is lost, which does not help to improve the accuracy of the results after machine learning.
Among other honorific tasks, such as the task of judging the correctness of honorific use, Shirado et al. (2011) constructs a set of rules for evaluating the appropriateness of misused honorific expressions based on subject-verb-object and some grammatical features of honorifics to help judge the appropriateness of honorific use, which can help identify the social relationship between the speaker and the hearer, but still missing information about the different degrees of respect of honorifics. Due to the limitations of automatically extracting linguistic knowledge based on grammatical rules, it is impossible to obtain deep knowledge from a corpus with tags of shallow information or the original corpus. This also leads to challenges in data annotation or data collection due to the subjective nature of language style compared to other NLP tasks such as question answering (Xu, 2017). A possible solution is to assign deep information tags to the corpus depending on the intended use of the linguistic resources. To address this problem, in this study, we present a corpus with the information based on systemic functional linguistics.

| SFL | Meaning | Annotation labels in KeiCO corpus |
|---|---|---|
| Field | What we want to talk about. | Field |
| Tenor | The social relationship between the participants in a conversation. | Honorific level<br>Respectful 尊敬語<br>Humble 謙譲語<br>Polite 丁寧語 |

Table 1: Field-Tenor-Mode Framework in SFL

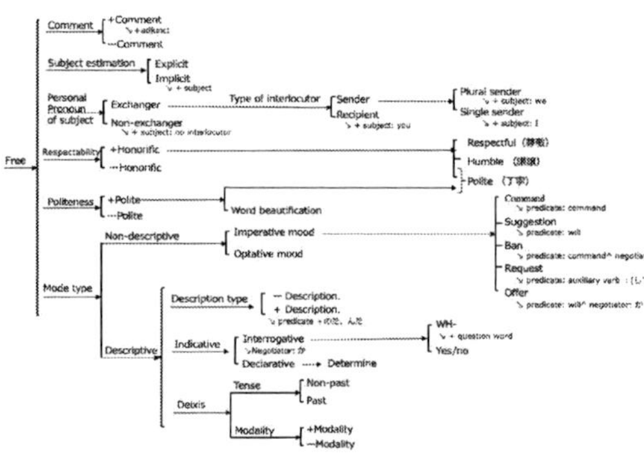


Figure 1: System Network of Mode system

## 3. Systemic Functional Linguistics

In Systemic Functional Linguistics (SFL, refer to appendix Appendix A for details), a language system is a concentric hierarchy of different types of symbolic systems - semantics, lexico-grammar, and phonology - surrounded by a context. It is a comprehensive model for the representation of language use in situations based on the values and common senses of a social group (Refer to Appendix: Figure 2). The context layer defines situations under three characteristics: the field, which describes the area of language use; the tenor, which describes the social relations between speakers; and the mode, which describes the medium used.
The characteristics are shown in Table 1. There are three meta-functions in the language system corresponding to each of the three properties of the context: ideational, interpersonal, and textual meanings, which constrain the selection of linguistic resources from the selection system network, called "system network", to form utterances appropriate to the situation.
In this study, we annotate each sentence with those mentioned above contextual elements of the three meta-functions to obtain the latent information necessary for language generation.
In particular, the annotation tags of the KeiCO corpus are defined based on the features of the system net-

work of mode system (Refer to Figure 1) in the lexico-grammatical layer reflecting interpersonal meanings.

## 4. The KeiCO Corpus

In the construction of the KeiCO corpus, we collected the original texts containing honorific expressions from the dictionary (Sakamoto and Nishikata, 2009), the articles on the internet, and crowdsourcing services. Furthermore, we crowdsourced about 40 native Japanese annotators to annotate the level of honorific expressions and other SFL features. Each annotator was assigned about 75 source texts and asked to rewrite them into other honorific levels as much as possible while maintaining the meaning of the source texts. We have allowed annotators to do nothing if they have difficulty in rewriting. After completing the annotation part, we asked another 20 native Japanese speakers to check the annotations and manually correct any errors in the corpus. After all annotating and checking, we got the result: 10,007 sentences in total and 5 annotations per sentence.

More details on annotation are shown in the following Section 4.1, and detailed corpus analysis is in Section 5.

### 4.1. Structure and Annotation

In the KeiCO corpus, each sentence is annotated with seven annotations: honorific level, respectful (尊敬語), humble (謙譲語), polite (丁寧語) and field. Detailed definitions are given below.

The Table 2 gives an overview of the KeiCO corpus. The first row shows the annotations for the features of the system network in the mode system.

For each corpus sentence in the first column, apart from the honorific level, each annotation is assigned to a value of 0 or 1, where 1 corresponds to the target attribute and 0 indicates the opposite. A detailed definition of each annotation is given in the 4.1 chapter.

#### 4.1.1. Honorific Level

The choice of honorifics primarily reflects role relationships (tenor). Tenor includes social, interpersonal relationships such as hierarchical relationships based on social status (e.g., boss-subordinate, teacher-student, etc.) and relationships (e.g., friend, acquaintance, etc.). In the KeiCO corpus, we set up four honorific levels reflecting the tenor. Each level is defined as follows.

**Level 1: The Highest Honorific Level** Level 1 is the level of respect most commonly used in the news, very formal speeches, and formal business emails. In sentences at the highest level of respect, it is common for verbs to be transformed into respectful or humble forms according to Japanese grammatical rules and for words that are originally respectful. It could also be a form of honorific linking, combining respectful (尊敬語) and humble (謙譲語) forms.

**Level 2: Secondary Honorific Level** Level 2 is widely used in business letters, general academic and business speeches, and the service industry. According to grammatical rules, the verb is transformed into respectful or humble, but few honorific linking forms are used.

**Level 3: Third Honorific Level** Complicated verb inflections are not used, and at most times, only polite (丁寧語) or word beautification (美化語) are used.

**Level 4: No Honorifics Used** No honorifics are used at all. Level 4 is more informal than Level 3 and may include polite expressions, abbreviations, and internet terminology.

#### 4.1.2. Respectful, Humble and Polite

Based on the features of the system network in the mode system, we use three kinds of honorific expressions as annotations: respectful, humble, and polite. Respectful expressions express the speaker's respect for the subject of the conversation and are used for actions, objects, and names of the respected person. Modest speech indicates the speaker's intention to show respect to the listener by lowering his or her words and actions. Polite speech is mainly used to encourage helping verb endings such as "desu（です）" and "masu（ます）" to beautify the topic and show respect for the language.

#### 4.1.3. Field

The field of activity indicates the area of use of the language, which includes the situation of having a conversation or the topic of the conversation. The use of honorifics is influenced by the specific activity field, such as business documents or lectures. To take this into account, In the KeiCO corpus, annotations are given to indicate specific activity areas. Currently, the KeiCO corpus has 122 different fields as options. (Refer to Appendix: Table 6)

## 5. KeiCO Corpus Analysis

### 5.1. Statistics of KeiCO

To analyze the use of vocabulary in KeiCO, we counted the number of sentences, the average sentence length, the average Kanji used in each sentence, the number of word tokens, word types and Yule's characteristic K. The characteristic statistics of KeiCO are shown in Table 3.

The $K$-characteristic was proposed by Yule (Yule, 1944). The smaller the value, the more diversity the vocabulary has. The $K$ characteristic value assumes that the occurrence of words follows a Poisson distribution. Here, $N$ means the number of word tokens and $V(m, N)$ means the number of word types that occur $m$ times in a dataset. The $K$ characteristic value is defined by the following equation 1.

$$K = 10^4 \times \frac{\sum_{all\,m}\left[m^2 V(m,N)\right] - N}{N^2} \quad (1)$$

In Table 3, the $K$ characteristic value decreased with the increase of the honorifics level, except for level 2. In fact, this exception is due to the fact that the number of sentences in honorifics level 2 is smaller than in other

Table 2: Overview of the KeiCO corpus

| Sentences from KeiCO corpus | Honorific level | Respectful 尊敬語 | Humble 謙譲語 | Polite 丁寧語 | Field |
|---|---|---|---|---|---|
| 本日は、かねてより相談したいことがあり、参上しました. (I have come here today to discuss something that I have been wanting to discuss for some time.) | 1 | 0 | 1 | 0 | 相談 consult |
| 今日は、折り入ってご相談したいことがあって伺ったのですが. (I came here today because I wanted to ask you about something.) | 2 | 0 | 1 | 0 | 相談 consult |
| 今日は相談したいことがあったため、来ました. (I came here today because I had something I wanted to discuss.) | 3 | 0 | 0 | 1 | 相談 consult |
| 今日はずっと相談したいことがあって来た. (I came here today to consult with you about something.) | 4 | 0 | 0 | 0 | 相談 consult |
| ⋮ | ⋮ | ⋮ | ⋮ | ⋮ | ⋮ |

Table 3: Statistical results of KeiCO

| Honorific level | Sentences | Average sentence length | Average Kanji in one sentence | Word tokens | Word types | Yule's characteristic $K$ |
|---|---|---|---|---|---|---|
| Level 1 | 2584 | 18.2 | 2.6 | 47111 | 4744 | 135.70 |
| Level 2 | 2046 | 16.4 | 2.1 | 33476 | 3897 | 136.23 |
| Level 3 | 2694 | 15.2 | 1.8 | 40980 | 4448 | 130.28 |
| Level 4 | 2683 | 13.5 | 1.6 | 36233 | 4315 | 129.80 |
| Total | 10007 | 15.8 | 2.0 | 157806 | 6465 | 125.54 |

levels. Regarding vocabulary, we confirmed that the use of Kanji increased with the honorific level.

## 5.2. KeiCO-based Classification

Since the advent of BERT (Devlin et al., 2019), BERT has achieved excellent performance in many tasks, making it one of the researchers' most commonly used models. In this section, we use BERT to perform a classification task, one of the most common and fundamental tasks, on our corpus KeiCO to examine how our corpus can improve performance in the NLP tasks.

To create a classification model, we use the KeiCO corpus to fine-tune the pre-trained BERT$_{BASE-Japanese}$[1], which was developed by Tohoku University. We divided the KeiCO corpus data into training, validation and evaluation in the ratio 6 : 2 : 2, respectively. The number of epochs was set to 30.

We randomly select sentences from the corpus in the ratio 1%, 10%, 100% (100, 1000, and 10007 sentences) to check the effect of the data quantity on the classification accuracy. Table 4 shows the average of the classification accuracy (10 times) for each extracting ratio and each annotation of the KeoCO corpus.

As a result, respectful (尊敬語), humble (謙譲語), and polite (丁寧語) yielded high classification accuracy, while honorific level yielded relatively low accuracy.

On the other hand, looking at the average increase rate with a tenfold increase in the data, we can find honorific level, respectful (尊敬語) and polite (丁寧語) yielded high, while humble (謙譲語) yielded relatively low on the increase rate.

**Respectful (尊敬語), Polite (丁寧語)** Grammatical features of respectful (尊敬語), polite (丁寧語) are expressed obviously in sentences, and models can quickly identify those features. Therefore, it is easy to get high classification accuracy and average increase rate.

**Humble (謙譲語)** We consider the classification model, which caused the low average accuracy increase rate, could not be trained well, because humble (謙譲語) is biased toward one label in the corpus (Refer to Table 5).

**Honorific Level** As mentioned in Section 4.1.1, the honorific levels are categorised into four levels; therefore, it is natural to assume that the accuracy of the task is lower than other binary classification tasks. The high accuracy increase rate is also due to the balanced number of levels in the corpus, which contributes to the improvement of the accuracy increase rate of the task.

[1]https://huggingface.co/cl-tohoku/bert-base-japanese

Table 4: Classification accuracy of each feature in the KeiCO corpus (10 times average)

| Classification accuracy | Honorific level | Respectful 尊敬語 | Humble 謙譲語 | Polite 丁寧語 |
|---|---|---|---|---|
| data using 1% | 0.482 | 0.646 | 0.894 | 0.706 |
| data using 10% | 0.653 | 0.686 | 0.887 | 0.810 |
| data using 100% | 0.727 | 0.698 | 0.906 | 0.842 |
| Average accuracy increase rate | 23.4% | 17.3% | 0.7% | 9.4% |

Table 5: Percentage of each annotation in the KeiCO corpus

| Honorific level1 | Honorific level2 | Honorific level3 | Honorific level4 | Respectful 尊敬語 | Humble 謙譲語 | Polite 丁寧語 |
|---|---|---|---|---|---|---|
| 26% | 20% | 27% | 27% | 39% | 9% | 24% |

## 6. Conclusion

Based on the language use taking social roles into account presented in systemic functional linguistics, we have created the KeiCO corpus, a corpus of Japanese honorifics that reflects the social status of speakers and listeners. The KeiCO corpus is annotated to take into account the social roles of dialogue participants in different domains of activity, as well as their modes of communication. As a general-purpose language resource, the corpus is expected to be useful for various tasks, such as improving the accuracy of machine translation, automatic evaluation, correction of Japanese composition and style transformation. We have not yet addressed the following issues: (1) The number of short sentences in each label is not balanced, (2) We need to review how copious the vocabularies are. Because some complex nouns are left intact in the rewritten sentences, which does not reflect the diversity of the vocabulary. In the future, we will increase the number of short sentences in the KeiCO corpus and put our main focus on the rewriting of nouns.

## 7. Bibliographical References


Aapakallio, N. (2021). Understanding through politeness–translations of japanese honorific speech to finnish and english. Master's thesis, Itä-Suomen yliopisto.

Danescu-Niculescu-Mizil, C., Sudhof, M., Jurafsky, D., Leskovec, J., and Potts, C. (2013). A computational approach to politeness with application to social factors. In *Proceedings of the 51st Annual Meeting of the Association for Computational Linguistics (Volume 1: Long Papers)*, pages 250–259, Sofia, Bulgaria, August. Association for Computational Linguistics.

Devlin, J., Chang, M.-W., Lee, K., and Toutanova, K. (2019). BERT: Pre-training of deep bidirectional transformers for language understanding. In *Proceedings of the 2019 Conference of the North American Chapter of the Association for Computational Linguistics: Human Language Technologies, Volume 1 (Long and Short Papers)*, pages 4171–4186, Minneapolis, Minnesota, June. Association for Computational Linguistics.

Feely, W., Hasler, E., and de Gispert, A. (2019). Controlling Japanese honorifics in English-to-Japanese neural machine translation. In *Proceedings of the 6th Workshop on Asian Translation*, pages 45–53, Hong Kong, China, November. Association for Computational Linguistics.

Jin, D., Jin, Z., Hu, Z., Vechtomova, O., and Mihalcea, R. (2020). Deep learning for text style transfer: A survey. *CoRR*, abs/2011.00416.

Liu, G., Yang, Z., Tao, T., Liang, X., Li, Z., Zhou, B., Cui, S., and Hu, Z. (2022). Don't take it literally: An edit-invariant sequence loss for text generation.

Madaan, A., Setlur, A., Parekh, T., Poczos, B., Neubig, G., Yang, Y., Salakhutdinov, R., Black, A. W., and Prabhumoye, S. (2020). Politeness transfer: A tag and generate approach. In *Proceedings of the 58th Annual Meeting of the Association for Computational Linguistics*, pages 1869–1881, Online, July. Association for Computational Linguistics.

Niu, T. and Bansal, M. (2018a). Polite dialogue generation without parallel data. *CoRR*, abs/1805.03162.

Niu, T. and Bansal, M. (2018b). Polite dialogue generation without parallel data. *Transactions of the Association for Computational Linguistics*, 6:373–389.

Rao, S. and Tetreault, J. (2018). Dear sir or madam, may I introduce the GYAFC dataset: Corpus, benchmarks and metrics for formality style transfer. In *Proceedings of the 2018 Conference of the North American Chapter of the Association for Computational Linguistics: Human Language Technologies, Volume 1 (Long Papers)*, pages 129–140, New Orleans, Louisiana, June. Association for Computational Linguistics.

Resmi, P. and Naseer, C. (2019). A deep learning approach for polite dialogue response generation. In *proceedings of the International Conference on Systems, Energy Environment (ICSEE) 2019*.

Sakamoto, T. and Nishikata, K. (2009). *A dictionary for honorific expressions ("Keigo no Ojiten" in Japanese)*. Sanseido.

Shirado, T., Marumoto, S., Murata, M., and Isahara, H. (2011). System for flexibly judging the misuse of honorifics in japanese. In *Proceedings of the 25th Pacific Asia Conference on Language, Information and Computation*, pages 503–510.

Tsai, A., Oraby, S., Perera, V., Kao, J.-Y., Du, Y., Narayan-Chen, A., Chung, T., and Hakkani-Tur, D. (2021). Style control for schema-guided natural language generation. In *Proceedings of the 3rd Workshop on Natural Language Processing for Conversational AI*, pages 228–242, Online, November. Association for Computational Linguistics.

Xu, W. (2017). From shakespeare to twitter: What are language styles all about? In *Proceedings of the Workshop on Stylistic Variation*, pages 1–9.

Yule, G. U. (1944). *The Statistical Study of Literary Vocabulary*. Cambridge: At the University Press.


## 8. Language Resource References


Klimt, B. and Yang, Y. (2004). The enron corpus: A new dataset for email classification research. In *European Conference on Machine Learning*, pages 217–226. Springer.

## Appendix A. Systemic Functional Linguistics

Systemic Functional Linguistics (SFL) is a linguistic theory established by M.A.K. Halliday, who was influenced by the ideas of Malinowski, a cultural anthropologist, and Firth of the London School of Linguistics, who studied under Firth.

The major difference between SFL and other linguistics is that SFL introduces context, including the cultural background of a social group, into its theory and examines the language system from the viewpoint of its function in society, while most linguistics avoid dealing with various meanings comprehensively, limit the treatment of language meanings, and focus on the aspect of grammar. In contrast, SFL introduces a context that includes the cultural background of a social group into its theory, and examines the language system from the perspective of its function in society. The language system represented by SFL is shown in Figure 2.

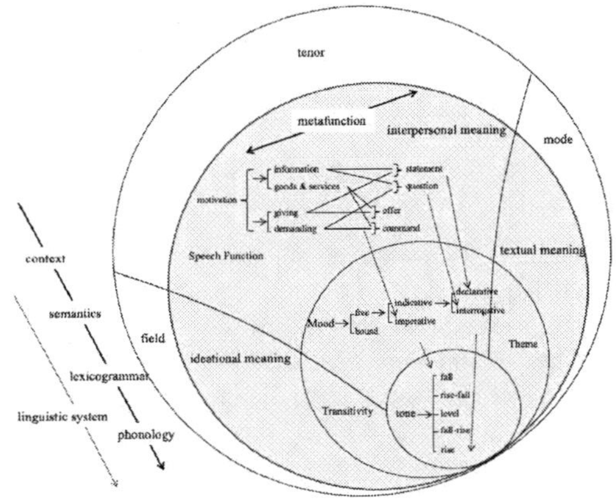


Figure 2: Language systems by systemic functional linguistics

Each layer of the language system expresses constraints on the choice of language resources through a network of choices called a choice network. The layers are organically connected by constraints called "realization statements". The systematization of linguistic resources using SFL and the procedures for their selection were considered to be directly applicable as algorithms for sentence generation, and in the 1980s they were called "systemic grammars" and used as the main linguistic theory for natural language sentence generation.

Table 6: List of fields in KeiCO corpus

| Rank | Field | Num. | Rank | Field | Num. | Rank | Field | Num. | Rank | Field | Num. | Rank | Field | Num. |
|---|---|---|---|---|---|---|---|---|---|---|---|---|---|---|
| 1 | email | 527 | 26 | enjoy | 112 | 51 | calculation | 60 | 76 | go back | 56 | 101 | self | 49 |
| 2 | food | 329 | 27 | control | 105 | 52 | seasons | 60 | 77 | seek | 56 | 102 | creation | 49 |
| 3 | money | 326 | 28 | like | 103 | 53 | advice | 60 | 78 | shop | 56 | 103 | aspiration | 49 |
| 4 | guest | 234 | 29 | write | 101 | 54 | application | 60 | 79 | recommend | 56 | 104 | ruling | 49 |
| 5 | buy | 229 | 30 | work | 100 | 55 | ask | 59 | 80 | recognize | 56 | 105 | beliefs | 49 |
| 6 | attitude | 227 | 31 | celebrate | 80 | 56 | gather | 59 | 81 | ask | 56 | 106 | chastisement | 48 |
| 7 | apologize | 217 | 32 | anger | 74 | 57 | see | 59 | 82 | exist | 56 | 107 | clothes | 47 |
| 8 | contact | 173 | 33 | letter | 66 | 58 | ideas | 59 | 83 | visit | 55 | 108 | review | 46 |
| 9 | gift | 162 | 34 | say | 64 | 59 | consider | 59 | 84 | announcement | 55 | 109 | praise | 46 |
| 10 | greeting | 159 | 35 | baby | 62 | 60 | physique | 59 | 85 | body | 55 | 110 | appease | 46 |
| 11 | questions | 158 | 36 | play | 62 | 61 | research | 59 | 86 | farewell | 55 | 111 | appear | 45 |
| 12 | political speech | 158 | 37 | invitation | 61 | 62 | sports | 58 | 87 | rejection | 55 | 112 | walk | 43 |
| 13 | words | 156 | 38 | life | 60 | 63 | acquire | 58 | 88 | experience | 55 | 113 | go out | 43 |
| 14 | home | 136 | 39 | surprisingly | 60 | 64 | hate | 58 | 89 | free | 54 | 114 | congratulate | 40 |
| 15 | notice | 134 | 40 | win | 60 | 65 | refute | 58 | 90 | help | 54 | 115 | confirm | 40 |
| 16 | reception | 120 | 41 | plan | 60 | 66 | escape | 58 | 91 | thanks | 54 | 116 | encourage | 40 |
| 17 | relations | 120 | 42 | refrain | 60 | 67 | Manage | 58 | 92 | heart | 53 | 117 | anxious | 37 |
| 18 | work | 120 | 43 | send | 60 | 68 | do | 58 | 93 | preparation | 53 | 118 | embarrassed | 37 |
| 19 | public | 119 | 44 | contract | 60 | 69 | socialize | 58 | 94 | return | 53 | 119 | disagree | 36 |
| 20 | concern | 117 | 45 | wear | 60 | 70 | wait | 57 | 95 | report | 52 | 120 | talk | 36 |
| 21 | secret | 116 | 46 | physical condition | 60 | 71 | take in | 57 | 96 | medical condition | 52 | 121 | change | 31 |
| 22 | seat | 116 | 47 | choose | 60 | 72 | entrust | 57 | 97 | anxiety | 51 | 122 | introduce | 24 |
| 23 | phone | 116 | 48 | teaching | 60 | 73 | Get in trouble | 57 | 98 | humble | 51 | | | |
| 24 | school | 116 | 49 | flattery | 60 | 74 | end | 57 | 99 | know | 50 | | | |
| 25 | death | 114 | 50 | consultation | 60 | 75 | disappointed | 57 | 100 | visit | 50 | | | |

## Appendix B. Ethical Considerations and Broader Impact

The corpus is collected through the crowdsourcing platform Lancers`https://www.lancers.jp` and has been stripped of any information in the text that might be specific to the individual, such as gender, sexual orientation, health status, etc. All private information such as the name and address of the person appearing in the text has been anonymised.

Due to the presence of offensive content in the least honorific sentences, we removed uncomfortable content such as sexual topics, excessive swearing, and allegedly discriminatory statements by manually checking the samples. Although differences in language use due to gender and age were not taken into account in the design of this corpus for the time being, we tried to have multiple (three or more) native Japanese speakers annotate the same sentence during the data collection phase, and later calculated the average of each annotation as the final determined value. This was done in order to reproduce, as far as possible, the most common and accepted language expressions in everyday life.

## Appendix C. Data Statement

We record information about our dataset following the data statement format proposed by Bender and Friedman (2018).
**Data set name:**KeiCO Corpus
**Data set developer:**Muxuan Liu
**Dataset license:**Creative Commons Attribution- NonCommercial-ShareAlike 4.0 International (CC BY- NC-SA 4.0)
**Link to dataset:** `https://github.com/Liumx2020/KeiCO-corpus`

### Appendix C.1. Curation Rattionale

We provide a corpus of Japanese honorifics with information on social stance and attempt to reflect specific Japanese honorific usage and levels of respect through label. The corpus consists of sentences from the dictionary (Sakamoto and Nishikata, 2009), the articles on the internet, and crowdsourcing services. As the generalizability of the dataset has not been tested for the time being, we didn't actively split the corpus into a training, development and test set, but rather encouraged the data to be split randomly by a certain percentage when performing machine learning tasks.

### Appendix C.2. Language Variety

N/A

### Appendix C.3. Speaker Demographic

No detailed information was collected regarding the demographics of the authors of the collected sentences. However, we only collected the text or the speech from Japanese native speaker.

### Appendix C.4. Annotator Demographic

The annotators are all Japanese native speaker but anonymous from internet, and no restrictions on age, gender or job.

### Appendix C.5. Speech Situation

See table 6

### Appendix C.6. Text Characteristics

The sentences in this dataset come from the dictionary (Sakamoto and Nishikata, 2009), the articles on the internet, and crowdsourcing services.

### Appendix C.7. Recording Quality

N/A

### Appendix C.8. Other

N/A

### Appendix C.9. Provenance Appendix

The dictionary (Sakamoto and Nishikata, 2009), the articles on the internet, and crowdsourcing services.

*Proceedings of the 1st Workshop on Dataset Creation for Lower-Resourced Languages (DCLRL) @LREC2022*, pages 27–35
Marseille, 24 June 2022


# Building an Icelandic Entity Linking Corpus

**Steinunn Rut Friðriksdóttir[1], Valdimar Ágúst Eggertsson[3], Benedikt Geir Jóhannesson[2], Hjalti Daníelsson[3], Hrafn Loftsson[2], Hafsteinn Einarsson[1]**
[1]University of Iceland, [2]Reykjavík University, [3]Quick Lookup
Reykjavík, Iceland
[1]{srf2, hafsteinne}@hi.is, [2]{benediktj20, hrafn}@ru.is, [3]{valdimar, hjalti}@snjallgogn.is

**Abstract**

In this paper, we present the first Entity Linking corpus for Icelandic. We describe our approach of using a multilingual entity linking model (mGENRE) in combination with Wikipedia API Search (WAPIS) to label our data and compare it to an approach using WAPIS only. We find that our combined method reaches 53.9% coverage on our corpus, compared to 30.9% using only WAPIS. We analyze our results and explain the value of using a multilingual system when working with Icelandic. Additionally, we analyze the data that remain unlabeled, identify patterns and discuss why they may be more difficult to annotate.

**Keywords:** Corpus Construction, Entity Linking, Named Entity Disambiguation, Information Extraction

## 1. Introduction

In recent years, Natural Language Processing (NLP) has progressed rapidly. New solutions in NLP have led to more effective human-computer interaction and easier access to on-demand knowledge (Balog, 2018). Before this development, the analysis of unstructured data posed a severe challenge if attempted without significant human input and domain knowledge. As a result, there has been growing interest in developing methods to work efficiently with unstructured data.

Information Extraction (IE) is the process of automatically retrieving structured information from unstructured, machine-readable sources. Such structured information can, for example, refer to Named Entities (NEs) found in any given text, the relationship between different entities, and the attributes that describe them. IE enables much deeper and more complex queries for such information from a far wider variety of sources (Sarawagi, 2008).

Prior work within the field of IE has focused on methods to recognize entities in text, which is known as Named Entity Recognition (NER). NER methods aim to automatically recognize NEs in text and assign them to appropriate predefined categories, like `Person`, `Organization` and `Location`. However, mentions can often be ambiguous and refer to different real-world entities depending on their context. For instance, a NER system does not differentiate between *Barack* and *Michelle* when both are referred to as *Obama*. This example demonstrates the need for Entity Linking (EL) and Named Entity Disambiguation (NED)[1]. After the NER task, the EL system looks the entities up in a Knowledge Base (KB), either a first-party one that has been created for the EL task, or a third-party one, such as Wikidata, and links their mentions to records in the KB. If multiple records are found for a given mention, the NED system performs disambiguation to select the correct entity based on the given context. The EL task is complete when the NEs have been disambiguated and correctly linked to the KB.

Building systems for NED and EL using state-of-the-art methods requires training data, i.e. a sufficiently large text corpus where mentions have been linked to correct entities in a KB. Building such a corpus and a KB can demand a significant effort, since it requires the labelling of mentions, the creation of entities in a KB, and the task of linking mentions to their corresponding records. The effort required can be a barrier to developing good NED and EL systems. Therefore, it is essential to develop methods that reduce the work required to create the training data.

In this paper, we present a method we used to efficiently build the first Icelandic corpus where entities are linked to corresponding records in a KB[2]. The underlying data is based on texts from diverse sources and is essential for any type of NED work in Icelandic as international corpora and KBs do not successfully reflect local entities and country-specific information. We believe that the method presented in this paper can be beneficial to those who want to bootstrap EL corpora for other lower-resource languages where entities are linked to the Wikidata KB.

The rest of this paper is structured as follows. In Section 2, we discuss previous work in the field of EL, particularly in relation to multilingual systems, and explain their significance to our work. In Section 3, we present our corpus and the methodology used for its compilation. Section 4 analyses our corpus as well as the performance of the methods used for its creation. We analyze the data that remain unlabeled in Section

[1]It should be noted that these terms are often used interchangeably. Some refer to the entire process as Entity Linking.

[2]Our corpus has been made publicly available on CLARIN-IS: `https://repository.clarin.is/repository/xmlui/handle/20.500.12537/168`

5 and explain which factors might cause difficulties in the labeling process.

## 2. Related work

Most publicly available EL corpora use Wikidata as a KB (e.g. Hoffart et al. (2011), Nuzzolese et al. (2015), and Minard et al. (2016)). The focus has been on text diversity in recent years, since training on professionally curated corpora, such as news articles, may not generalize well to other domains, such as text from social media. For example, Eshel et al. (2017) compiled their EL corpus by crawling the web searching for links to Wikipedia. This way, they constructed the WikilinksNED corpus, which consists of Wikipedia hyperlinks and their surrounding context, using page IDs as unique identifiers for entities. As another example, Botzer et al. (2021) presented an EL corpus of 17,316 entities collected from Reddit, manually annotated by Mechanical Turk workers who matched mentions to Wikipedia links.

Most work in the field of EL has focused on English, but multilingual EL has received increased attention in the last 10 years or so. Originally, most multilingual EL systems linked mentions in a specific language or languages to a KB in another, higher-resource language such as English (e.g. McNamee et al. (2011), Mayfield et al. (2011), Ji et al. (2015)). In contrast, Botha et al. (2020) proposed a method where language-specific mentions are linked to a language-agnostic Wikipedia-based KB. Their model covers over 100 languages and 20 million entities, making the EL process more inherently multilingual. Following their lead, De Cao et al. (2021) presented a sequence-to-sequence system, mGENRE, for multilingual EL, which is the system we use in our corpus generation process.

mGENRE is a multilingual version of the GENRE model (De Cao et al., 2020), trained on large corpora in 125 languages and covering a range of $\sim$730M Wikipedia hyperlinks in 105 languages. The model is an auto-encoder based on the BART architecture (Lewis et al., 2020). For a given input text, mGENRE generates language IDs and entity names that, in combination, uniquely identify records in the Wikidata KB. Importantly, mGENRE does not require an external KB at runtime since information about entities is contained in its trained network parameters. Furthermore, by maintaining entity names in as many languages as possible, mGENRE is able to exploit connections between languages along with interactions between the source mention context and the target entity name. During inference, beam search is used to determine the probability scores for candidates. The scores for different languages are marginalized in order to score entities (De Cao et al., 2021). It is worth noting that mGENRE performs EL and NED simultaneously.

In this work, mGENRE is used to suggest records in Wikidata to speed up the EL labeling process in an Icelandic corpus. We would like to emphasize that, as Icelandic is one of the 105 languages covered by mGENRE, the model can be applied directly to our data. Thus, a replication of this study, for the other languages that mGENRE covers, should be eminently feasible. The corpus is based on an annotated NER corpus, MIM-GOLD-NER (Ingólfsdóttir et al., 2020a), which contains around 48,000 NEs (Ingólfsdóttir et al., 2020b). The corpus is tagged for eight NE types (`Person`, `Location`, `Organization`, `Miscellaneous`, `Date`, `Time`, `Money` and `Percent`) and is in the CoNLL format. We advance MIM-GOLD-NER to the next logical step by building a new corpus, MIM-GOLD-EL, in which NEs of type `Person`, `Location`, `Organization`, and `Miscellaneous` from MIM-GOLD-NER are linked to unique entities in the Wikidata KB.

Icelandic Language Technology (LT) has made notable advances recently, not least in relation to a national funding program aimed at creating the necessary resources for further advancement in the field (Nikulásdóttir et al., 2020; Nikulásdóttir et al., 2021). This has resulted in the publication of multiple LT tools and resources during the last three years or so, which has brought Icelandic into a medium-resource language tier. We benefit greatly from the fact that the MIM-GOLD-NER corpus has already been published, making our work significantly easier. While Icelandic does not technically qualify as a low-resource language[3] anymore, we still believe that our work can be considered beneficial for languages in need of EL data, particularly those that are covered by mGENRE. As mGENRE builds on Wikipedia as a foundation, we note that efforts to build Wikipedia in a given language can lead to downstream benefits such as better EL in models such as mGENRE.

## 3. Corpus compilation

In order to create our corpus, MIM-GOLD-EL, we started by preprocessing MIM-GOLD-NER in accordance with the input format required for mGENRE. For each entity, mGENRE generates a set of identifiers (IDs) that consist of pairs of the language in question and the name of the entity in said language. Each Wikidata item has a set of Wikipedia pages in multiple languages linked to it, thus the task of mGENRE is to uniquely identify the entities using these IDs. We ran the data through mGENRE, which proposed Wikidata IDs for the retrieved entities and set them as labels for the mentions. We checked our results manually, accepting or rejecting each of the model's predictions. This resulted in 46.6%, of the 39,793 mentions examined, being accepted.

Subsequently, we ran all mentions through a separate process, which we refer to as Wikipedia API Search (WAPIS). In this process, we used the text of each

[3] A low-resource language is a language for which few online resources exist or for which few computational data exist (Cieri et al., 2016).

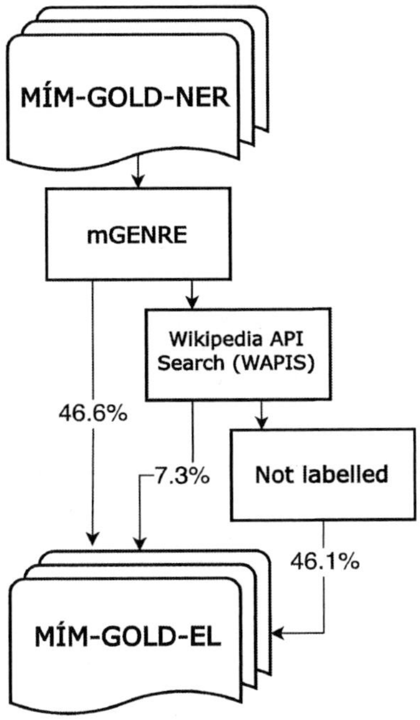


Figure 1: Our corpus compilation process with proportions of mentions retrieved for each step, i.e. 46.6% of all mentions are labeled by mGENRE and subsequently 7.3% of all mentions are labeled using the WAPIS. Of all mentions, 46.1% were not identified and were marked as `unlabeled` label in MIM-GOLD-EL.

mention in a search query run on the Wikipedia API, specifically the Icelandic and the English wikis. The query is the equivalent of entering the full text of the mention into a Wikipedia search window, and harvesting the suggested links that would appear below in a drop-down list. For each such query, we used the full text of the mention, unaltered (e.g. not lemmatized) and not including any surrounding context in the source texts.

Mentions that had remained unlabeled after the mGENRE round, and had acquired at least one Wikipedia link after the WAPIS, had their set of links manually reviewed. If one of those links was a match for the mention, we marked that link as the correct label, with preference given to Icelandic links whenever possible. Out of the full set of all mentions, only 7.3% were found by WAPIS but not by mGENRE[4]. Mentions that were neither covered by mGENRE nor WAPIS are also a part of our dataset and may be distinguished from the linked mentions. We cover these mentions in the next two sections and discuss why they might remain unlabeled[5].

Our purpose with WAPIS was twofold: First, to see if we could increase the amount of correct labels for our mentions, and, secondly, to evaluate mGENRE's overall output when compared to that of a simple Wikipedia text search. It turned out that WAPIS did increase the amount of correct labels, and mGENRE outperformed WAPIS. As noted above, mGENRE's results resulted in 46.6% of mentions being accepted. The subset of those accepted mentions that also had the correct label in the subsequent WAPIS was 23.6% (these were not manually reviewed, since the correct candidate had already been established). The entirety of mentions confirmed by WAPIS, irrespective of whether they'd been labeled earlier by mGENRE, was 30.9%, while the total coverage of our combined approaches of mGENRE and WAPIS was 53.9%. The process is illustrated in Figure 1. Finally, using these results we conclude that mGENRE's accuracy on labeled entities in our corpus is 86.4%[6].

Figure 2, shows the ratio of mentions covered by our methods for each NER type. The `Location` type is the most easily retrieved by our methods, followed by `Organization` and `Miscellaneous`. The lowest scoring category is that of `Person`. This is most likely due to how many of the unlabeled mentions refer to people or fictional characters that do not have a corresponding Wikidata entry. On the other hand, locations are generally well documented and infrequently lack their corresponding entries. The `Miscellaneous` category includes mentions that refer to products, books and movie titles and events.

The overall process was completed in approximately one month and performed by four annotators. mGENRE was run using a GeForce RTX 2070 SUPER 16GB. No specific computational power is needed for WAPIS.

## 4. Exploratory Corpus Analysis

It is apparent when examining the results that context-aware language models (like mGENRE) provide significant improvements over a plain search query lookup. Using only the WAPIS would have resulted in only a 30.9% coverage rate. Additionally, there are significant benefits in using multilingual EL methods when working with low-resource languages. Our entities are retrieved from Wikipedia pages in 68 different languages. As shown in Figure 3, the most common languages are Icelandic and English which constitute 81.3% and 6.2% of the entities retrieved

[4]Due to the nature of our approach, we did not study a WAPIS-only process since it would have resulted in a significant amount of additional work. However, we note that languages not covered by mGENRE but with a sizeable Wikipedia, could benefit from a WAPIS-only approach.

[5]Note that a mention is only marked as unlabeled in the released data if both the *suggestion wiki* (WAPIS-only result) and *correct wiki* (mGENRE result) fields are empty, indicating that neither of our methods were successful.

[6]This is calculated by dividing the number of words labeled by mGENRE by the number of words labeled by both methods

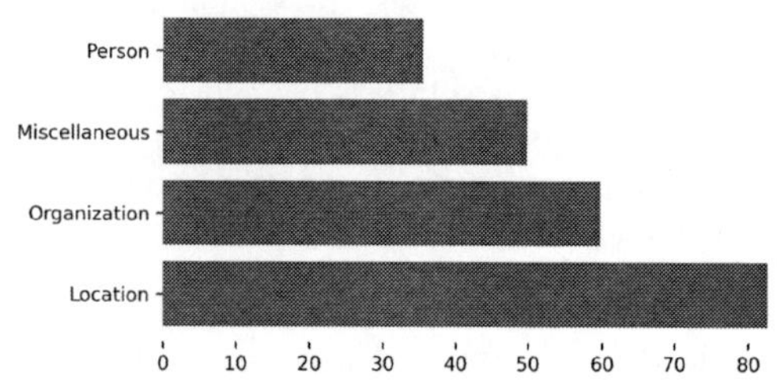


Figure 2: Ratio of mentions retrieved by our methods for each NER type.

by mGENRE, respectively. Other languages therefore account for 12.8% of the retrieved entities. While it is apparent that Icelandic makes up the majority of all retrieved entities (75.3% of the entities retrieved by the WAPIS were also from the Icelandic Wikipedia), it is still safe to assume that our coverage rate would have been significantly lower if we had restricted ourselves to the Icelandic Wikipedia.

It's worth noting that using a model such as mGENRE might introduce some biases. Looking at Figure 3, we see that the most common languages beside Icelandic and English are Swedish (1.3%), French (1.3%), Japanese (1%), German (0.8%) and Norwegian (0.6%). Most of these languages are close to Icelandic, both in a cultural and linguistic sense, particularly the Nordic languages. Additionally, at the time of writing, the French edition of Wikipedia has the third largest number of articles published and the German edition has the seventh[7]. While it might seem slightly surprising to see Japanese among these languages, it should be noted that most mentions retrieved by the Japanese Wiki were actually Japanese car models. In any case, having all these languages as available resources significantly improves the coverage rate.

As can be seen in Figure 4, the performance of mGENRE and WAPIS is quite varied for different text subcategories in our corpus. The lowest performance was in the books category where only 38.2% of mentions were linked to their corresponding entities. This is explained by the fact that a lot of the fictional characters who appear in these books do not have Wikidata entries, and by the nature of the way books are written, these types of mentions appear very frequently in the text. It is a bit surprising how high the blog category scores as it includes plenty of mentions that lack proper context for disambiguation and might refer to people that are not public figures. It is also interesting that there is a significant difference in performance for the two newspaper categories, Fréttablaðið at 64.2% and Morgunblaðið at 46.9%. Currently, we do not have an explanation for this difference. It is, however, apparent that the highest scoring categories are generally those that have most likely been proofread, the highest scoring of which is the adjudications,[8] followed by the Icelandic Web of Science, an academic page run by the University of Iceland.

We analyzed our results in accordance with the fact that Icelandic is a morphologically rich language. In this analysis, each word is treated individually, thus multiword mentions are treated as multiple words. The total number of words examined was 56,732, out of which 38,674 were nominals (including 36,874 nouns). Foreign words were 14,370. In Figure 5, the coverage rate of each morphological category can be seen. It is clear that the overall trend is in line with the overall coverage rate of our methods: mGENRE reaches approximately 7% less coverage than the combined methods (the difference ranges from 2.26% to 14.4%, excluding the ungendered nouns where the difference is 23.3%) and does not appear to struggle with any morphological category in particular. Our analysis thus indicates that mGENRE shows great potential when used for morphologically rich languages.

While our methods have reached a decent coverage rate, there remains a lot of room for improvement as 46.1% of our data remain unlabeled. Table 1 shows some examples of the words not retrieved by our methods. We find that relying solely on Wikipedia and on Wikidata as a KB, even with 125 different language versions available, falls significantly short of complete coverage. Some improvements could be made by automatically creating new Wiki entries for the mentions that do not exist in the KBs. This would certainly work for well-known people, fictional characters and locations that coincidentally do not already have their own entry. However, that does not solve everything as can clearly be seen within our blog subcategory. There, it is essentially impossible to disambiguate a lot of the mentions, as they refer to common people and the context of the text might be long forgotten. How to solve the EL task for noisy data such as from social media therefore still remains an open question in this context.

## 5. Analysis of the Remaining Data

As illustrated in Figure 1, 46.1% of the mentions were not covered by the first two steps of the process, mGENRE and WAPIS. Looking at the remaining unlabeled data, we see some patterns. First, some of the mentions are either specific to Icelandic context or infrequent in everyday language. These mentions do not have a corresponding Wikipedia record and therefore cannot be discovered by the first two steps of the process. Second, it is difficult to properly disam-

[7] See the list of Wikipedias wiki page.

[8] It should be noted that the adjudications texts include anonymized names (both for persons and locations) so the coverage rate is skewed by the fact that if the text contains the pseudonym A, we mark it as a correct label if our methods suggest a Wiki entry about the letter A. This category is included because it is a part of the original corpus but needs significant revisions to be useful for EL purposes.

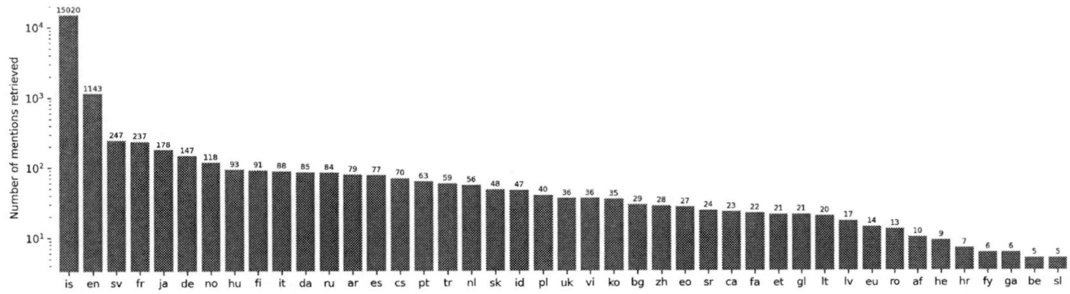


Figure 3: Number of mentions retrieved by mGENRE per language. The majority of mentions retrieved were in Icelandic (81.3%) followed by English (6.2%) and Swedish (1.3%). Languages with fewer than five linked records are omitted.

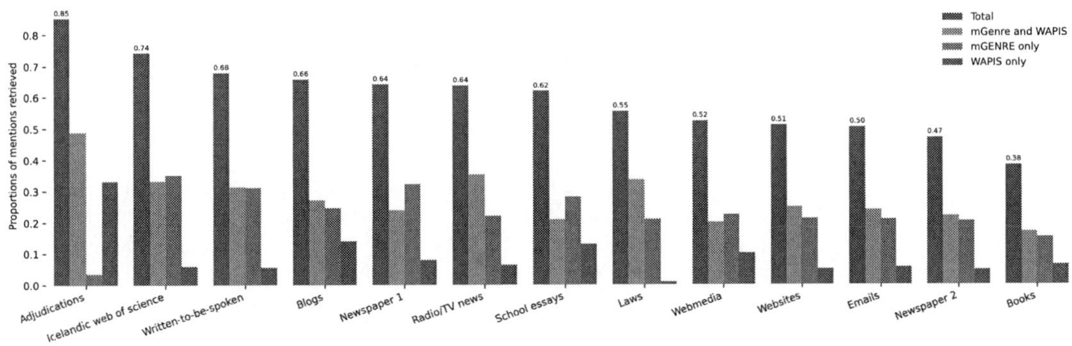


Figure 4: Proportions of mentions retrieved per text subcategory in the MIM-GOLD-NER corpus.

biguate last names by themselves, particularly when they are used for reference (e.g. in parenthetical referencing in academic text, mostly found in articles from the Icelandic Web of Science). In most cases, last names will not be retrieved by the WAPIS method either, as it assumes that the mention refers to a first name. Third, abbreviations prove difficult in most cases, except when the entity is more commonly referred to by its abbreviation than its actual name (e.g. NASA). Examples of these types of non-retrieved mentions can be found in Table 1.

We manually examined the remaining data in order to gain a better understanding of what type of data specifically causes our methods to fail to return a label. Out of the 18,402 unlabeled entities, 7,236 or 39.3% refer to a person (most commonly academics, musicians, and athletes) and 2,706 or 14.7% refer to a fictional character. Institutions and companies make up 12.4% of the unlabeled data, particularly noticeable of which are churches and public institutions that have abbreviations (e.g. *Landspítalinn* (the largest public hospital in Iceland) often gets referred to as *LSH*). Locations take up 10.1%, most commonly street names, clubs, restaurants or farms. Among the categories that account for less than 3% of the unlabeled data are book titles, brands, events, radio and TV shows, nomenclatures and magazine titles. Interestingly enough, there are also 28 mentions of God (particularly when referred to as *the Lord*) that our methods do not cover.

While examining these categories, we also annotated the data based on specific factors that might impact the model's ability to decipher their meaning. 4,826 or 26.2% of all mentions refer to a person using only their first name, which is almost invariably done with Icelandic names unless they are appearing for the first time in a given text. On the other hand, 730 or 4% of the mentions refer to a person only by their last name, and nicknames account for 4.3%. Other factors that can misdirect our methods from retrieving labels for peoples' names is when there is an insertion between the first and the last name (i.e. *Halldór* ***heitinn*** *Laxness*, '***the late*** *Halldór Laxness*'). We considered several other factors such as abbreviations (4%), a total lack of context (1.2%), inexact locations such as *Asian countries* (0.7%) and Icelandic translations of foreign titles (0.5%).

Clearly, there are a lot of components to consider when using automatic methods for entity linking. While the process is made a lot quicker and simpler by the

| Icelandic | Translation | Probable reason for non-retrieval |
|---|---|---|
| Vesturlandabúans | Inhabitant of the Western countries | Low frequency, oblique case. No specific Wiki entry. |
| Borginni | The City | Oblique case, refers to a diner/club that doesn't exist anymore. No specific Wiki entry. |
| Aðalbygging | The Main Building (refers to the main building of the University of Iceland) | A common moniker, no specific Wiki entry. |
| Jóni Hjaltalín Ólafssyni | A doctor's name | Oblique case, this person does not have a Wiki entry. |
| Mersault | Meursault (French Wine) | The name is misspelled in our data. |
| Bjössi | A name of a fictional character | A common nickname of a person, this book character does not have a Wiki entry. |
| Jón | A person's name (refers to Jón Steinsson, economist) | A common name of a person which, standing by itself, lacks context for disambiguation. |
| Forliti | A person's last name | Stands by itself in a parenthetical reference, lacks context for disambiguation. |
| Svarta kortið | The Black Card (a credit card for students) | Low frequency, no Wiki entry. |
| Swann | A person's last name (refers to Charles Swann, fictional character) | Stands by itself, lacks context for disambiguation. |
| Barnið | An Icelandic translation of the Belgian movie title, L'Enfant | Translated movie titles hardly ever get their own Wiki entries. L'Enfant does not have an entry in the Icelandic Wikipedia. |
| Steinar | A person's name (the text refers to 'Steinar bóndi í Hlíðum', meaning a farmer from a specific farm that has a relatively generic name) | Could refer to multiple people, little chance of disambiguation without more context. |
| Digranesvegi | A street name | Oblique case, no specific Wiki entry. |
| Herdísar L. Storgaard | A nurse's name | Oblique case, this person does not have a specific Wiki entry. |
| Ólafur Gísli Jónsson | A person's name | This person does not have a specific Wiki entry. |
| Miðausturland | The middle of the East side of Iceland | Very specific, yet non-specific location. No Wiki entry. |
| EÖÞ | Abbreviation of an author's name | Stands by itself. Very hard to disambiguate without more context. |

Table 1: Examples of mentions not retrieved/labeled by our methods and proposed explanations for the failure.

use of language models that greatly reduce the need for manual annotation, they still fall short in many cases where a human annotator might not have any difficulties reaching the correct conclusion. As previously stated, however, a part of the problem is that when relying solely on Wikidata as a KB, we can never reach full coverage, particularly on entities that appear very rarely. For rare entities with unique names, this is not a problem, but once disambiguation is required, the task can become significantly more challenging, even for a person with access to an online search engine. In such cases, it is not clear what the entity should be linked to. One way to approach this problem is to provide some reference, like a web link to a record in an archive that can be considered a good source for that item. Another approach could be to build a larger Wikipedia, possibly via some form of automation. While such approaches may be promising, they present several challenges, especially concerning validation. We emphasize that references to rare entities outside existing knowledge bases is an important unsolved problem and we do not cover it further in this paper.

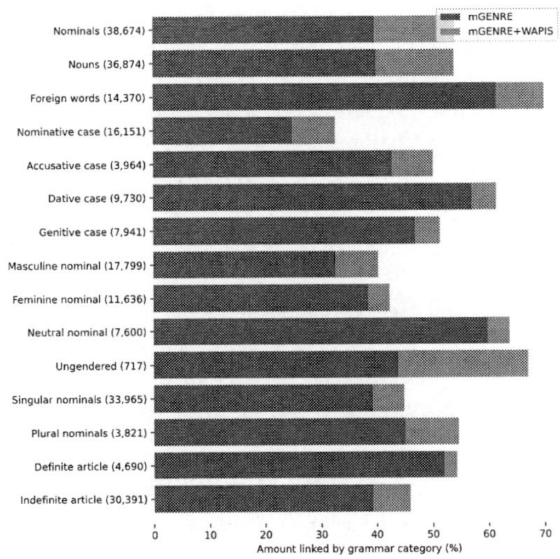


Figure 5: Proportions of mentions retrieved per morphological category in the MIM-GOLD-NER corpus. The total number of words for each category is shown within brackets.

## 6. Ethical Considerations and Broader Impact

When working with language data, it is important to consider the ethical implications of one's work. In the context of entity linking, this includes ensuring that the data used to train and test entity linking models is representative of the real-world distribution of entities, and that the entities in the data are linked correctly and accurately. Furthermore, in the case of the Icelandic entity linking dataset, the data was partially collected from public websites such as blogs without the consent of the individuals involved. While the data is public, it is possible that some individuals may not want their data to be used for research purposes.

Entity linking datasets can have a broad impact beyond the immediate research context in which they are used. For example, a dataset of entities linked to Wikipedia pages could be used to improve search results for a given entity, or to generate summaries of entities for a given user. Furthermore, a dataset of entities linked to named entities could be used to improve the accuracy of named entity recognition models, which is an important component of many natural language processing applications.

## 7. Conclusion

Icelandic is a morphologically rich language with its own sets of challenges when it comes to creating an EL system. No training data has previously existed for this purpose and thus the first milestone in our journey has been the creation of an EL corpus, MIM-GOLD-EL, which is based on an existing NER corpus, MIM-GOLD-NER. We used mGENRE, a sequence-to-sequence EL model, in order to label our corpus and improved our results using Wikipedia API Search. We analyzed our methodology with regards to reducing manual labour and examined how the morphology of Icelandic can be a factor in our results. Furthermore, we presented a detailed analysis on the data not covered by our methods.

Future milestones will include the creation of a comprehensive and open knowledge graph (KG) of Icelandic NEs which is an essential foundation of most EL projects as well as NED related research and development. Additionally, we will adapt a proven, state-of-the-art technology in order to create an Icelandic Entity Linker, the first of its kind.

## 8. Acknowledgments

This work was funded by the Icelandic Strategic Research and Development Program for Language Technology 2021, grant no. 200075-5301.

## 9. Bibliographical References

Balog, K. (2018). Entity-Oriented Search, volume 39 of The Information Retrieval Series. Springer.

Bender, E. M. and Friedman, B. (2018). Data statements for natural language processing: Toward mitigating system bias and enabling better science. Transactions of the Association for Computational Linguistics, 6:587–604.

Botha, J. A., Shan, Z., and Gillick, D. (2020). Entity Linking in 100 Languages. arXiv preprint arXiv:2011.02690.

Botzer, N., Ding, Y., and Weninger, T. (2021). Reddit Entity Linking Dataset. Information Processing & Management, 58(3):102479.

Cieri, C., Maxwell, M., Strassel, S., and Tracey, J. (2016). Selection criteria for low resource language programs. In Proceedings of the Tenth International Conference on Language Resources and Evaluation (LREC'16), pages 4543–4549, Portorož, Slovenia, May. European Language Resources Association (ELRA).

De Cao, N., Izacard, G., Riedel, S., and Petroni, F. (2020). Autoregressive Entity Retrieval. arXiv preprint arXiv:2010.00904.

De Cao, N., Wu, L., Popat, K., Artetxe, M., Goyal, N., Plekhanov, M., Zettlemoyer, L., Cancedda, N., Riedel, S., and Petroni, F. (2021). Multilingual Autoregressive Entity Linking. arXiv preprint arXiv:2103.12528.

Eshel, Y., Cohen, N., Radinsky, K., Markovitch, S., Yamada, I., and Levy, O. (2017). Named Entity Disambiguation for Noisy Text. arXiv preprint arXiv:1706.09147.

Hoffart, J., Yosef, M. A., Bordino, I., Fürstenau, H., Pinkal, M., Spaniol, M., Taneva, B., Thater, S., and Weikum, G. (2011). Robust disambiguation of named entities in text. In Proceedings of the

2011 Conference on Empirical Methods in Natural Language Processing, pages 782–792.

Ingólfsdóttir, S. L., Guðjónsson, Á. A., and Loftsson, H. (2020b). Named Entity Recognition for Icelandic: Annotated Corpus and Models. In International Conference on Statistical Language and Speech Processing, pages 46–57. Springer.

Ji, H., Nothman, J., Hachey, B., and Florian, R. (2015). Overview of TAC-KBP2015 Tri-lingual Entity Discovery and Linking. In Lecture Notes in Computer Science.

Lewis, M., Liu, Y., Goyal, N., Ghazvininejad, M., Mohamed, A., Levy, O., Stoyanov, V., and Zettlemoyer, L. (2020). BART: Denoising sequence-to-sequence pre-training for natural language generation, translation, and comprehension. In Proceedings of the 58th Annual Meeting of the Association for Computational Linguistics, pages 7871–7880, Online, July. Association for Computational Linguistics.

Loftsson, H., Yngvason, J. H., Helgadóttir, S., and Rögnvaldsson, E. (2010). Developing a pos-tagged corpus using existing tools. In 7th SaLTMiL Workshop on Creation and use of basic lexical resources for less-resourced languages LREC 2010, Valetta, Malta, 23 May 2010 Workshop programme, page 53.

Mayfield, J., Lawrie, D., McNamee, P., and Oard, D. W. (2011). Building a cross-language entity linking collection in twenty-one languages. In International Conference of the Cross-Language Evaluation Forum for European Languages, pages 3–13. Springer.

McNamee, P., Mayfield, J., Lawrie, D., Oard, D. W., and Doermann, D. (2011). Cross-language Entity Linking. In Proceedings of 5th International Joint Conference on Natural Language Processing, pages 255–263.

Minard, A.-L., Speranza, M., Urizar, R., Altuna, B., Van Erp, M., Schoen, A., and Van Son, C. (2016). Meantime, the newsreader multilingual event and time corpus. In Proceedings of the Tenth International Conference on Language Resources and Evaluation (LREC'16), pages 4417–4422.

Nikulásdóttir, A. B., Guðnason, J., Ingason, A. K., Loftsson, H., Rögnvaldsson, E., Sigurðsson, E. F., and Steingrímsson, S. (2020). Language Technology Programme for Icelandic 2019-2023. In Proceedings of the Twelfth International Conference on Language Resources and Evaluation (LREC 2020), pages 3414–3422, Marseille, France.

Nikulásdóttir, A. B., Þórunn Arnardóttir, Guðnason, J., Þorsteinn Daði Gunnarsson, Ingason, A. K., Jónsson, H. P., Loftsson, H., Óladóttir, H., Sigurðssona, E. F., Þór Sigurgeirsson, A., Snæbjarnarson, V., and Steingrímsson, S. (2021). Help Yourself from the Buffet: National Language Technology Infrastructure Initiative on CLARIN-IS. In Proceedings of the CLARIN Annual Conference.

Nuzzolese, A. G., Gentile, A. L., Presutti, V., Gangemi, A., Garigliotti, D., and Navigli, R. (2015). Open knowledge extraction challenge. In Semantic Web Evaluation Challenges, pages 3–15. Springer.

Sarawagi, S. (2008). Information extraction. Foundations and Trends® in Databases, 1(3):261–377.

## 10. Language Resource References

Ingólfsdóttir, S. L., Guðjónsson, Á. A., and Loftsson, H. (2020a). MIM-GOLD-NER – named entity recognition corpus (2021-09-29). CLARIN-IS.

## A. Data statement

This statement follows the schema proposed by Bender and Friedman (2018).

**Dataset name:** MIM-GOLD-EL

**Dataset developer:** Steinunn Rut Friðriksdóttir, Valdimar Ágúst Eggertsson, Benedikt Geir Jóhannesson, Hjalti Daníelsson.

**Dataset license:** IGC-Corpus License[9]

**Link to dataset:** `https://repository.clarin.is/repository/xmlui/handle/20.500.12537/168`

### A.1. Curation rationale

As stated in Section 2 and 3, MIM-GOLD-EL is an extension of the previously available MIM-GOLD-NER corpus which is itself an extended version of the MIM-GOLD corpus (Loftsson et al., 2010). MIM-GOLD-EL consists of over 21,000 mentions that have been linked to their corresponding Named Entities in Wikidata and is intended as training material for Icelandic or multilingual EL models.

The original MIM-GOLD corpus is intended as a gold standard for Icelandic POS-taggers. It consists of one million words of text that were tagged automatically and then manually corrected. The text was compiled from various sources as illustrated in 2 (MIM-GOLD, MIM-GOLD-NER and MIM-GOLD-EL all contain the exact same text with different annotations) which should ensure that it is generalizable and not limited to a specific domain.

As noted in Footnote 8, one of the files from the original MIM-GOLD corpus contains adjudications where entities representing people and locations have been anonymized. This file is only included in MIM-GOLD-EL to respect the original schema and is not well suitable for EL tasks.

### A.2. Language variety

The language of this corpus is Icelandic. No dialect specifications apply to Icelandic.

[9]https://repository.clarin.is/repository/xmlui/page/license-gigaword-corpus

### A.3. Speaker demographic

Due to the nature of the corpus, it's hard to give detailed information regarding the demographics of the authors. We can infer that all of the text were written by Icelandic authors aged between 18-70.

### A.4. Annotator demographic

The four annotators that worked on MIM-GOLD-EL were all Icelandic, aged between 28-42. One of the annotators has a degree in Icelandic and three are computer scientists. All of the annotators have extensive professional proficiency in computational linguistics.

### A.5. Speech situation

The corpus is divided into several subsections that include various types of language registers. The language used in the texts compiled from news articles is not the same as that of the blogs despite Icelandic having no dialects. However, all of the text presented in the corpus is written text (as opposed to transcriptions of speech).

### A.6. Text characteristics

Same applies here as with the speech situation. The text presented in the corpus is compiled from various sources and thus contains various characteristics.

### A.7. Recording quality

N/A

### A.8. Other

N/A

### A.9. Provenance appendix

See Section 2 and 3.

*Proceedings of the 1st Workshop on Dataset Creation for Lower-Resourced Languages (DCLRL) @LREC2022*, pages 36–43
Marseille, 24 June 2022


# Crawling Under-Resourced Languages – A Portal for Community-Contributed Corpus Collection

**Erik Körner[1,2], Felix Helfer[2], Christopher Schröder[1], Thomas Eckart[2], Dirk Goldhahn[2]**
[1]Leipzig University, Leipzig, Germany,
[2]Saxon Academy of Sciences and Humanities, Leipzig, Germany,
erik.koerner@uni-leipzig.de

**Abstract**

The "Web as corpus" paradigm opens opportunities for enhancing the current state of language resources for endangered and under-resourced languages. However, standard crawling strategies tend to overlook available resources of these languages in favor of already well-documented ones. Since 2016, the *Crawling Under-Resourced Languages portal* (CURL) has been contributing to bridging the gap between established crawling techniques and knowledge about relevant Web resources that is only available in the specific language communities. The aim of the CURL portal is to enlarge the amount of available text material for under-resourced languages thereby developing available datasets further and to use them as a basis for statistical evaluation and enrichment of already available resources. The application is currently provided and further developed as part of the thematic cluster "Non-Latin scripts and Under-resourced languages" in the German national research consortium Text+. In this context, its focus lies on the extraction of text material and statistical information for the data domain "Lexical resources".

**Keywords:** CURL, Community-Contributed, Corpus Creation, Dataset Creation, Web Crawling

## 1. Introduction

Despite various endeavors over the last decades to decrease the gap between well and under-resourced languages, the current situation of language documentation and the availability of language resources for the latter are still unsatisfactory. This is even acknowledged by the UN, which proclaimed the years 2022 – 2032 as the International Decade of Indigenous Languages (IDIL[1]), thereby showing that a global effort and a large variety of stakeholders are necessary for the "preservation, revitalization and promotion" of indigenous languages. Work in this area can only be fruitful and sustainable when local language communities are directly involved in all crucial parts of the process and when all general principles of responsible scientific work are considered. These include policies like the CARE Principles for Indigenous Data Governance[2] but also the general FAIR principles.

Following the "Web as corpus" paradigm (Kilgarriff and Grefenstette, 2003), the aim of the *Crawling Under-Resourced Languages portal* (CURL portal) is to collect Web-based text resources and make them publicly available for everyone. Contrary to explorative Web crawls, the source domains are provided by users via the CURL portal, thereby allowing anyone to collaborate. The resulting web crawls are then processed into datasets which include the pre-processed plain text, i.e. the raw text extracted from HTML that has been cleaned and subsequently segmented into sentences and tokens. The sentences are randomly shuffled to not allow reconstruction of the original documents (see also Appendix A.1. on copyright and license). Moreover, these datasets contain metadata, such as lists of visited Web domains, word co-occurrences and word frequencies. The gathered material is also used to constantly improve applications in Natural Language Processing (NLP), and is offered and employed by projects such as the Leipzig Corpora Collection (LCC) (Goldhahn et al., 2012).

During the last 6 years, the portal was introduced to and discussed with native speakers of different under-resourced and indigenous language communities. Such participation is crucial to obtain Web links containing under-resourced languages. Most of these links are difficult to find using standard Web crawling techniques, and often cannot be handled well by standard NLP components such as language detectors that rely on training data. The former affects – among others – .com domains where relevant material is hard to identify in case of inadequate language detection or domains that are only sparsely linked to and therefore often ignored by popular Web search engines.

The CURL portal allows anyone to contribute to the creation of digital and openly available language resources with minimal effort and a very low barrier of entry. Especially in cases where direct exchange and knowledge transfer "on site" is hard to achieve (e.g. because of organizational or financial reasons) the portal is an easy-to-use alternative.

## 2. Related Work

The CURL portal is being developed and maintained since 2016 and has been continuously revised and improved since then. Previous publications focused on planning and implementation (Goldhahn et al., 2016) or on presenting first use cases (Goldhahn et al., 2017)

[1]https://en.unesco.org/idil2022-2032
[2]https://www.gida-global.org/care

rather than providing a bigger picture of the portal, its acceptance by language communities and its purpose to foster availability of text datasets and lexical resources, all oh which is discussed in this work. CURL is part of the Leipzig Corpora Collection (Goldhahn et al., 2012) and is built upon its technology such as the processing pipeline for corpora creation or various forms of data access (including different web portals or web services). CURL is part of the LCC's strategy to offer large monolingual corpora for various languages; its results are therefore integrated into the LCC. Furthermore, the portal is part of the German national research consortium Text+ in the dedicated lexical cluster "Non-Latin scripts and Under-resourced languages"[3] which focuses on the creation and maintenance of lexical resources for those languages in a sustainable infrastructure.

Most work concerned with corpus collection and creation for under-resourced languages is invested by individual researchers who prepare a resource for a particular purpose or to answer a specific research question. A significant contribution to the more general collection of corpora for under-resourced languages was made by the An Crúbadán project (Scannell, 2007). Utilizing textual resources from highly multilingual sources and applying a BootCaT like approach (Baroni and Bernardini, 2004), corpora for various languages were created and extended with the help of language experts. Though typically very small, textual samples for a striking number of languages are provided.

Yet other projects are concerned with generic corpus creation without addressing the challenges of under-resourced languages such as LanguageCrawl (Roziewski and Stokowiec, 2016) which builds upon Common Crawl[4].

## 3. Web Portal & Corpus Creation

The central entry point for contributors is the CURL web page[5] where users can submit new URLs about a language to be processed. Moreover, users can browse a list of 285 languages, showing existing corpora, including statistics about corpora stemming from previous submissions and lists of URLs provided so far, making the whole process as transparent as possible.

New submissions only require selecting a language, identified by its ISO 639-3 code, and providing a list of URLs of web pages with text in the chosen language. In case a specific under-resourced language is not yet listed, the project can be contacted and will add it.

After submission, new jobs are run automatically. The main processing steps as show in Figure 1 include:

1. Crawling the URLs using the open-source web crawler Heritrix (Mohr et al., 2004) for up to 6 hours and being restricted to the provided domains,
2. Extracting all possible text content using jWarcEx[6] from the HTML documents,
3. Detecting the language of the text and filtering out documents not belonging to the target language,
4. Preprocessing documents into sentences with (1) sentence segmentation, (2) rule-based cleaning, (3) language separation on single sentences, and (4) sentence deduplication,
5. Merging with sentences from previous submissions and existing corpora,
6. Corpus creation using word tokenization and cooccurrence computation.

A contact email can be provided to be notified when all steps are completed. Completed corpora will be published on the CURL web page together with basic statistics about the number of word types, tokens, sentences, and sources; searchable lists of URLs and domains are also provided.

### Language Detection and Separation

Aside from the problem of missing seed URLs, lack of sufficient language material obstructs language identification since in particular under-resourced languages might not be supported by existing language detectors – and training a new model is only an option if sufficient data is available. Language detection is an essential step that cannot be omitted since (a) the URLs received from the CURL portal may contain text in multiple languages and (b) might also not contain the target language at all (for example if the crawler operates during a temporary downtime of the web site). To circumvent the problem of a missing initial model, we use bible and watchtower texts, which are available to us in about 1,000 languages combined and which have been successfully applied to similar scenarios before (Brown, 2013; Agić et al., 2016). Using a character n-gram based classification model (Brown, 2013), we identify the dominant language of each crawled document, filtering out all text material that is not in the language of interest while preserving text containing foreign or loan words.

After a successful submission to the CURL portal, we can use the resulting text data and create a new language detection model for the corresponding language. As a result, we can then either replace a previous bible and watchtower model or train an improved model on all data that has been crawled so far, thereby iteratively improving the detection of under-resourced languages. For languages with no available model, manual assistance is necessary. After filtering out textual data in other well known languages using the language detection setup described above, project staff checks the remaining texts and its sources using available web documentation and common sense. This ideally results in a first model for the language and eventually in its first dataset to be made available. The same holds for jobs

[3] https://textplus.org/en

[4] https://commoncrawl.github.io/cc-crawl-statistics/plots/languages

[5] https://curl.wortschatz-leipzig.de/

[6] https://github.com/Leipzig-Corpora-Collection/jwarcex

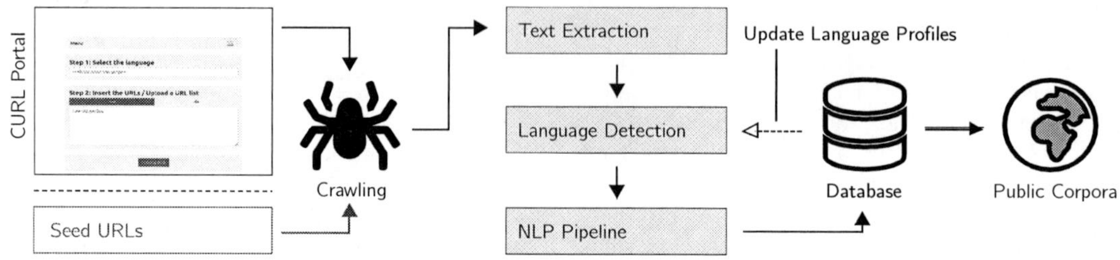


Figure 1: Overview of the full process from crawling to corpora. The lower path from "Seed URLs" to "Public Corpora" is a typical crawling setup, which is, however, infeasible for under-resourced languages with little to no URLs available. The CURL portal helps to alleviate this obstruction in a collaborative fashion. After successful completion of a new submission, the resulting database can be used to train a language detection model for detecting this language in other more general web crawls.

where despite crawling resulting in decent amounts of textual data and having a language model for the respective language, no data is classified to be of the desired language. Only by manually figuring out the reasons can this situation be resolved. Reasons can be, among others, a wrongly assigned language model or websites not actually containing the expected language.

## 4. Statistics

Between 2016 and 2022, 202 jobs were submitted for 134 languages. Most of these were successful and created new or augmented existing corpora.

### 4.1. Submissions

Some submissions unfortunately were not able to add new sentences since the corpora already contained those. 42 jobs failed due to various reasons such as crawling errors (page gone, blocked), text extraction (no content found, e.g. pages with JavaScript), or language detection/separation (e.g. page about the target language, not in the target language; e.g. text in English). If possible, it was tried to finish jobs manually, in particular when language detection failed because of insufficient models. In those cases, text segments with high confidence scores for languages such as English were filtered out and the process was continued focusing on the remaining material.

Table 1 shows submissions totaling at least 20 seed URLs and the number of sentences that could be extracted. While the number of URLs does not correlate with the number of extracted sentences after processing due to various reasons, submissions with higher numbers of URLs generally lead to text of the target language with a greater reliability than submissions with only a few (or a single) URL(s).

Submissions in 18 languages (*pes, sqi, nep, mkd, tat, glk, tam, hye, ben, tel, tgl, tgk, war, msa, ceb, uzb, bos, mal*) resulted in more than one million sentences.

| Language | | Submissions | URLs | Sentences |
|---|---|---|---|---|
| tsn | *(Tswana)* | 4 | 8,268 | 28,276 |
| ben | *(Bengali)* | 5 | 4,043 | 1,200,255 |
| zul | *(Zulu)* | 12 | 1,731 | 158,644 |
| nso | *(Northern Sotho)* | 5 | 455 | 9,560 |
| tso | *(Tsonga)* | 3 | 330 | 10,571 |
| wol | *(Wolof)* | 2 | 311 | 9,988 |
| ven | *(Venda)* | 2 | 294 | 9,279 |
| sna | *(Shona)* | 2 | 277 | 48,339 |
| xho | *(Xhosa)* | 8 | 184 | 63,387 |
| uig | *(Uyghur)* | 4 | 123 | 68,736 |
| bam | *(Bamanankan)* | 6 | 61 | 10,874 |
| ndo | *(Ndonga)* | 2 | 58 | 13,495 |
| run | *(Rundi)* | 6 | 49 | 17,361 |
| ckb | *(Central Kurdish)* | 2 | 44 | 4,978 |
| knn | *(Konkani)* | 2 | 38 | 14,111 |
| tgk | *(Tajiki)* | 3 | 36 | 939,144 |
| bcl | *(Central Bikol)* | 1 | 35 | 15,726 |
| kir | *(Kyrgyz)* | 1 | 32 | 251,608 |
| nbl | *(Southern Ndebele)* | 2 | 20 | 318 |

Table 1: The number of sentences, URLs, and submissions for languages with at least 20 submitted URLs.

### 4.2. Domains and TLDs

URLs of the domain `wikipedia.org` appeared in submissions of 99 languages. They are in the top-5 based on the amount of extracted sentences for 36 languages and the sole resource for 27 languages.

However, for 37 languages no jobs with Wikipedia URLs were submitted. Nine languages of those only contain a single domain, with the languages *dyu, fon, nyn, tem, tiv* having less than 20 sentences each and *kck, bak, gom,* and *nan* only having 1k, 3k, 40k, and 77k sentences, respectively.

The spread of domains per language varies. Disregarding single-domain languages, we found that the top-5 domains cover almost all the sources of sentences for a language. Exceptions being *ben, hye, kea, kng, knn, ngl,*

| Language | Proportion | Sentences |
|---|---|---|
| pes *(Iranian Persian)* | 47.8% | 3,980,346 |
| hye *(Armenian)* | 27.5% | 376,981 |
| sot *(Southern Sotho)* | 34.9% | 3,410 |
| knn *(Konkani)* | 15.0% | 2,124 |
| kea *(Kabuverdianu)* | 31.8% | 82 |
| snk *(Soninke)* | 46.1% | 57 |
| ngl *(Lomwe)* | 48.7% | 37 |
| kng *(Koongo)* | 46.4% | 19 |

Table 2: Number of sentences for top-5 domains with the proportion of sentences per domain less than 50%.

*pes, snk, sot*, with the top-5 only amounting to less than 50% (cf. Table 2).

The top TLDs across languages are: **.org** for 106 languages, most occurrences due to wikipedia.org, **.com** (80), **.net** (26), **.edu** (14). Surprisingly often, URLs come from country-code TLDs in which the respective language is not spoken natively. These include **.de** (33), **.pl** (24), **.nl** (18), **.ru** (18), **.jp** (17), **.cn** (16). This demonstrates that language resources are often 'hidden' on international TLDs and require assistance from native speakers to be found.

### 4.3. Examples

Particularly successful languages were:

**Rundi (*run*)**: After being contacted by language experts, we got 6 submissions with 49 URLs in total. Starting from 3k sentences, we currently have 17,361 sentences.

**Zulu (*zul*)**: After being contacted by language experts, we received 11 submissions with 1730 URLs in total. We currently have 146,216 sentences.

The languages **Bengali (*ben*)** with 1,200,255, **Tswana (*tsn*)** with 28,276, **Tsonga (*tso*)** with 10,571, **Venda (*ven*)** with 9,279, and **Xhosa (*xho*)** with 63,387 sentences can also be counted as successes as we got a variety of new domains (including **.com**) with the proportion of wikipedia being rather low (less than 20%). Table 3 shows the top-5 domains of those five languages. `wikipedia.org` is highlighted in italics.

| Lang. | Domain | Sentences | % |
|---|---|---|---|
| ben | http://www.jugantor.com/ | 126,841 | 10.7 |
| | http://www.anandabazar.com/ | 110,892 | 9.4 |
| | http://www.prothom-alo.com/ | 54,647 | 4.6 |
| | *http://bn.wikipedia.org/* | 34,698 | 2.9 |
| | http://www.guruchandali.com/ | 30,308 | 2.6 |
| tsn | http://www.mmegi.bw/ | 6,672 | 23.6 |
| | http://www.dailynews.gov.bw/ | 4,856 | 17.2 |
| | http://www.kutlwano.gov.bw/ | 4,528 | 16.0 |
| | *http://tn.wikipedia.org/* | 3,578 | 12.7 |
| | http://www.info.gov.za/ | 1,063 | 3.8 |
| tso | http://rivoni.org/ | 1943 | 18.4 |
| | http://globalrecordings.net/ | 1,579 | 15.0 |
| | http://oldgov.gcis.gov.za/ | 1,521 | 14.4 |
| | http://www.info.gov.za/ | 1,135 | 10.8 |
| | http://www.nthavela.co.za/ | 569 | 5.4 |
| ven | http://www.gov.za/ | 1,250 | 13.6 |
| | http://globalrecordings.net/ | 1,130 | 12.3 |
| | http://www.saqa.org.za/ | 1,119 | 12.2 |
| | http://info.hannasteffens.de/ | 780 | 8.5 |
| | http://africanlanguages.com/ | 518 | 5.6 |
| xho | http://www.wordpocket.com/ | 17,669 | 27.9 |
| | https://builttobrag.com/ | 10,249 | 16.2 |
| | http://nalibali.mobi/ | 5,266 | 8.3 |
| | *https://xh.wikipedia.org/* | 5,077 | 8.0 |
| | http://wced.school.za/ | 3,385 | 5.3 |

Table 3: Top-5 domains of sentences with amount and proportion (percentage of the whole corpus).

## 5. Discussion

As we have shown, the CURL portal is an accessible, uncomplicated tool for the collection and creation of text corpora for under-resourced languages that is actively used and can already provide resources for a significant number of different languages. These high-quality text corpora can in turn be freely used for further research and practical applications. For example, they can function as baseline corpora for a large number of NLP tasks, can serve as a basis for statistical analysis, can help improve language detection tools, and so on. The collected URLs may also be of use as seeds for further crawling processes for the respective language. First tests also show that the collected text material is suitable for enriching existing datasets (Bosch et al., 2018).

A worthwhile future addition to the CURL portal would be the training of word or character embeddings from the collected data. Word embeddings such as Word2Vec (Mikolov et al., 2013) and GloVe (Pennington et al., 2014), or contextual string embeddings like the Flair embeddings (Akbik et al., 2018) allow text to be represented in a semantically relevant, machine-interpretable way that has proven to be a valuable tool for a multitude of downstream NLP tasks. Trained models of such embeddings are unfortunately usually only available for a small number of well-resourced languages, making their creation for other languages a worthwhile goal, as this could enable new avenues for further research in the respective communities.

A community-driven endeavor like this is obviously very much dependent on external participation. We therefore also hope to strengthen our visibility to reach even more language communities interested in the contribution to and collaboration with this growing resource collection.

## Acknowledgements

This research was partially funded by the Development Bank of Saxony (SAB) under project numbers 100335729 and 100341518. It is being developed further in the German national research consortium (NFDI) Text+ in the lexical cluster "Non-Latin scripts and Under-resourced languages". Text+ is funded by the German National Research Foundation (DFG) under project number 460033370.

## 6. Bibliographical References


Agić, Ž., Johannsen, A., Plank, B., Martínez Alonso, H., Schluter, N., and Søgaard, A. (2016). Multilingual projection for parsing truly low-resource languages. *Transactions of the Association for Computational Linguistics*, 4:301–312.

Akbik, A., Blythe, D., and Vollgraf, R. (2018). Contextual string embeddings for sequence labeling. In *Proceedings of the 27th International Conference on Computational Linguistics*, pages 1638–1649, Santa Fe, New Mexico, USA, August. Association for Computational Linguistics.

Baroni, M. and Bernardini, S. (2004). BootCaT: Bootstrapping Corpora and Terms from the Web. In *Proceedings of the Fourth International Conference on Language Resources and Evaluation (LREC'04)*, pages 1313–1316. European Language Resources Association (ELRA).

Bender, E. M. and Friedman, B. (2018). Data statements for natural language processing: Toward mitigating system bias and enabling better science. *Transactions of the Association for Computational Linguistics*, 6:587–604.

Bosch, S., Eckart, T., Klimek, B., Goldhahn, D., and Quasthoff, U. (2018). Preparation and usage of Xhosa lexicographical data for a multilingual, federated environment. In *Proceedings of the Eleventh International Conference on Language Resources and Evaluation (LREC 2018)*, Miyazaki, Japan, May. European Language Resources Association (ELRA).

Brown, R. D. (2013). Selecting and weighting n-grams to identify 1100 languages. In Ivan Habernal et al., editors, *Text, Speech, and Dialogue - 16th International Conference, TSD 2013, Pilsen, Czech Republic, September 1-5, 2013. Proceedings*, volume 8082 of *Lecture Notes in Computer Science*, pages 475–483. Springer.

Goldhahn, D., Eckart, T., and Quasthoff, U. (2012). Building Large Monolingual Dictionaries at the Leipzig Corpora Collection: From 100 to 200 Languages. In *Proceedings of the Eighth International Conference on Language Resources and Evaluation (LREC'12)*, pages 759–765. European Language Resources Association (ELRA).

Goldhahn, D., Sumalvico, M., and Quasthoff, U. (2016). Corpus Collection for Under-Resourced Languages with More than One Million Speakers. *Proceedings of Collaboration and Computing for UnderResourced Languages: Towards an Alliance for Digital Language Diversity (CCURL)*, pages 67–73.

Goldhahn, D., Eckart, T., and Quasthoff, U. (2017). A Portal for Corpus Collection for Under-Resourced Languages. *Workshop of the African Association for Lexicography (AFRILEX)*, pages 15–17.

Kilgarriff, A. and Grefenstette, G. (2003). Introduction to the special issue on the web as corpus. *Computational Linguistics*, 29(3):333–348.

Mikolov, T., Chen, K., Corrado, G., and Dean, J. (2013). Efficient estimation of word representations in vector space. In *1st International Conference on Learning Representations, ICLR 2013*, Scottsdale, Arizona, USA.

Mohr, G., Stack, M., Ranitovic, I., Avery, D., and Kimpton, M. (2004). An Introduction to Heritrix – An open source archival quality web crawler. In *In IWAW'04, 4th International Web Archiving Workshop*. Springer Press.

Pennington, J., Socher, R., and Manning, C. D. (2014). Glove: Global vectors for word representation. In *Empirical Methods in Natural Language Processing (EMNLP)*, pages 1532–1543.

Roziewski, S. and Stokowiec, W. (2016). LanguageCrawl: A generic tool for building language models upon Common-Crawl. In *Proceedings of the Tenth International Conference on Language Resources and Evaluation (LREC'16)*, pages 2789–2793. European Language Resources Association (ELRA).

Scannell, K. P. (2007). The Crúbadán Project: Corpus building for under-resourced languages. *Cahiers du Cental*, 5:1.

# A. Ethical Considerations and Broader Impact

## A.1. Copyright and License

The CURL corpora are automatically collected from public sources contributed by third parties without considering the content of the contained text in detail. No responsibility is taken for the content of the data. In particular, the views and opinions expressed in specific parts of the data remain exclusively with the authors.

Only public web pages are being crawled, and page metadata that restricts crawling, e.g. `robots.txt`, is respected to not affect normal use of the websites and avoid downloading unauthorized content.

In the creation process of the text corpora, only unique sentences with their source reference are kept, but the original order in text is discarded, so no reconstruction of original documents is possible.

All corpora CURL and LCC provide for download are licensed under the Creative Commons license CC BY.[7]

## A.2. Impact

We do not expect the CURL corpora to have a significantly higher negative impact in terms of publication of personal data, copyright infringement, or systematic bias, compared to other publicly available web corpora. The web pages were crawled with open source tools (e.g. Heritrix) that allow anyone to download the same texts with consumer-grade computers. The full texts might also be contained and accessible in larger web crawls and collections such as `archive.org` or `commoncrawl.org`. To alleviate the likelihood of copyright and license infringement, the largest related text segments published are sentences.

We seek to lower the entry threshold for prospective new researchers by offering CURL as a free service for anyone to contribute to, thereby creating and making available the cleaned text corpora for academic research. This will allow anyone to quickly start working with and researching statistical properties of the corpora and various natural language-related tasks without first having to acquire raw texts and then build pipelines to prepare the data. The corpora contain monolingual sentences, cleaned and enriched with co-occurrence relations and statistical information, but can be used for further post-processing, including manual cleaning and annotation for various downstream tasks.

# B. Languages and TLDs

Table 4 presents the most frequent TLDs for all the sentence resources of the CURL portal combined. TLDs with less than 7 languages are cut off. In particular, the TLD **.com** has the highest number of sentence source domains across all 80 languages. The total number of sentences is about 35 million.

[7] `https://wortschatz-leipzig.de/en/usage`

# C. Tools

## C.1. Text cleaning

Text cleaning occurs multiple times in the process:

1. When extracting text from WARCs, filtering out text blocks shorter than a minimum line length (defaults to 20 characters) and documents with too few lines (defaults to 80),
2. when detecting the language of a document, to filter out documents where the majority language does not match the target language,
3. after sentence segmentation by using rule-based filters that employ empirical values for lengths, amounts of characters (e.g. punctuation), and regular expressions for certain undesirable patterns,
4. finally with language detection on the sentence level.

## C.2. Sentence Segmentation

For sentence segmentation we consider the following context information:

- List of possible sentence boundaries (or combinations), e.g. punctuation characters,
- tokens that should not occur in front of a sentence boundary (i.e. a list of abbreviations),
- patterns that should not occur in front of a sentence boundary (like typical year dates "[1-2][0-9]{3}"),
- tokens that should not occur immediately after a sentence boundary (like typical names for months),
- patterns that should not occur immediately after a sentence boundary (like a lowercase word).

Each language contains custom abbreviation lists, some of which include custom sentence boundaries or other configurations. For languages without sentence boundaries like Thai, third-party state-of-the-art segmentation tools are used.

Parameters and lists for different languages were refined by language experts and user feedback over time.

## C.3. Word Tokenization

Word tokenization for most languages employs a white-space tokenizer extended with rules about punctuation characters, abbreviations, and multi-word unit lists. Non-whitespace segmented languages are tokenized using third-party language-specific software.

# D. Data statement

We document the following dataset information about the CURL corpora collection according to the approach proposed by Bender and Friedman (2018).

**Dataset Name**: CURL – Crawling Under-Resourced Languages

**Dataset License**: Creative Commons license CC BY [7]

**Link to Dataset**: `https://curl.wortschatz-leipzig.de/languages`

### D.1. Curation Rationale

The CURL corpora are a collection of monolingual web text corpora. Seed URLs are community-contributed, with subsequent automated web crawling, text cleaning and corpus creation. The corpora include tokenized sentences, words, word co-occurrences and statistics, sources, and the relations in-between.
The aim of the CURL project is the discovery of digital text resources for under-resourced languages with the help of native speakers. The computed text corpora are made publicly available to support academic research.

### D.2. Language Variety

All CURL corpora are monolingual, identifiable by their ISO 639-3 code. The languages covered are listed by Goldhahn et al. (2016), with the current selection available on the CURL web page.[5]

### D.3. Speaker Demographic

It was not possible to collect and analyze detailed information about the demographic characteristics of the authors of the collected sentences due to the variety of languages and amount of texts. For the language skills, we assume native speaker proficiency levels and a high number of different authors.

### D.4. Annotator Demographic

N/A

### D.5. Speech Situation

Contemporary written language on web pages. No detailed information about topics was collected.

### D.6. Text Characteristics

Web texts, Wikipedia. From informal to formal. Varying text quality. No restrictions on topic.

### D.7. Recording Quality

N/A

### D.8. Other

**Curators**: Non-native speakers, ages between 25–65, female and male. Experts in computational linguistics, natural language processing and corpus creation, with extensive proficiency in German and English.
**Contributors** (of seed URLs and texts): Anonymous.

### D.9. Provenance Appendix

N/A

| TLD | Sentences | Domains | Languages |
|---|---|---|---|
| org | 6,900,832 | 755 | ace, ach, amh, anw, asm, aym, bam, ban, bcl, ben, bew, bjn, bod, bos, bug, cdo, ceb, che, chv, ckb, diq, ewe, ful, gan, glg, glk, grn, hat, hau, hye, ibo, ilo, jav, kab, kan, kas, kbd, kde, kea, khk, khm, kik, kin, kir, kng, knn, kon, ksw, kur, lao, lin, lug, mal, min, mkd, mkw, mlg, mos, msa, mya, mzn, ndo, nep, nso, nya, oci, ori, orm, pag, pam, pes, pnb, pnt, que, rom, run, sin, skr, sna, snd, snk, som, sot, sqi, sun, tat, tel, tgk, tgl, tha, tir, tsn, tso, tuk, tum, uig, uzb, ven, vls, war, wol, xho, ydd, yor, zha, zul |
| com | 15,548,196 | 88,885 | aar, ach, amh, bam, ban, bcl, bem, ben, bik, bos, ceb, ckb, diq, ewe, fon, glg, glk, gom, hat, hau, hil, hye, ibb, ibo, jav, kan, kck, kde, kea, khk, kin, kng, knn, kur, lao, lgg, lug, mal, mkd, mos, msa, mya, nep, ngl, nor, nso, nya, oci, orm, pag, pes, pnb, prs, run, seh, sin, skr, sna, snk, som, sot, sqi, suk, sun, swa, tam, tat, tel, tgk, tgl, tha, tsn, tso, tuk, ven, wol, xho, ydd, yor, zul |
| de | 39,010 | 288 | ban, bcl, bem, bos, ceb, ckb, diq, emk, fuc, glg, glk, hye, jav, kde, kea, khk, kin, knn, lgg, mos, msa, ngl, nya, oci, pes, seh, snk, som, suk, sus, tgl, tha, ven |
| net | 681,689 | 50 | ben, bod, bos, glg, glk, hye, kan, khk, kur, lao, lin, msa, ndo, nep, pes, run, sna, som, tel, tha, tsn, tso, ven, wol, xho, zul |
| pl | 1,112 | 143 | ach, ban, bcl, bos, ceb, diq, glg, hye, ibb, jav, kde, kea, kng, knn, lgg, msa, ngl, nya, oci, pes, seh, snk, som, tgl |
| cz | 1,562 | 429 | ban, bcl, bem, bos, diq, fuc, glk, hat, ibb, jav, kea, khk, kng, knn, ngl, nya, oci, pag, pam, pes, snk |
| se | 2,496 | 61 | ban, bem, bos, ckb, diq, glk, jav, kea, kng, knn, mos, nya, nyn, oci, pes, prs, snk, som, suk, tha |
| sk | 1,013 | 175 | ban, bcl, bem, bos, glg, ibb, jav, kde, kea, kng, knn, lgg, min, mos, ngl, nya, oci, pam, pes, seh |
| nl | 1,595 | 54 | bos, diq, glk, jav, kea, knn, mos, ngl, nya, oci, pes, snk, som, sus, tgk, tgl, tha, tiv |
| no | 50,661 | 75 | bos, ckb, diq, emk, glk, kea, knn, msa, nbl, nor, oci, pes, pnb, skr, sna, som, tgl, tir |
| ru | 12,205 | 179 | bak, bos, chv, ckb, glk, hye, jav, khk, kir, knn, nya, oci, pes, snk, tat, tem, tgk, tgl |
| ch | 513 | 74 | bos, ckb, diq, glk, jav, kde, kea, kin, kng, knn, msa, oci, pes, suk, sus, tgl, tha |
| in | 23,732 | 1,208 | ace, bem, bos, ceb, glk, jav, knn, lgg, mad, mal, msa, pes, pnb, skr, sun, tgl, tha |
| jp | 313 | 35 | bem, bos, hat, kde, kea, kng, knn, lgg, mos, msa, nya, pes, snk, suk, tgl, tha |
| cn | 26,541 | 27 | bem, bos, ceb, glk, hau, ibb, jav, khk, mos, msa, oci, pes, tgl, tha, uig |
| ir | 2,081,118 | 5,120 | bos, fuc, glk, hau, kir, knn, msa, pes, pnb, run, skr, tgk, tgl, tha, tuk |
| it | 734 | 85 | bcl, bem, bos, glg, hau, ibb, kea, knn, lgg, nya, oci, pes, seh, suk, tgl |
| dk | 923 | 32 | bos, ceb, ckb, diq, glk, ibb, jav, kea, mos, oci, pes, pnb, skr, som |
| edu | 5,607 | 37 | bcl, bik, glg, glk, hat, msa, pes, pnb, tgl, tha, wol, xho, ydd, zul |
| ca | 693 | 30 | bos, glk, hat, hau, hye, mos, msa, pes, pnb, snk, ssw, tgl, tha |
| co.za | 58,163 | 1,255 | bos, kng, nbl, nso, nya, pes, sot, ssw, tsn, tso, ven, xho, zul |
| fr | 4,616 | 103 | bos, glk, hat, hye, kng, knn, msa, oci, pes, run, snk, tha, zul |
| ro | 853 | 395 | ban, bcl, bos, diq, kea, knn, nya, oci, pag, pes, snk, suk, tgl |
| tr | 467 | 22 | bcl, ckb, emk, glk, jav, kde, knn, lgg, ngl, pes, snk, suk, tuk |
| tw | 76,877 | 25 | bos, hau, ibb, jav, kea, khk, kng, knn, mos, msa, nan, pes, tha |
| ee | 38 | 19 | bos, chv, glg, kir, lgg, mad, mos, ngl, nya, oci, snk, suk |
| za | 36,572 | 260 | knn, nbl, nso, nya, pes, sot, ssw, tsn, tso, ven, xho, zul |
| lt | 107 | 22 | ban, bos, glk, kde, kea, knn, lgg, mos, oci, pes, tgl |
| mobi | 10,781 | 10 | bos, hau, mos, msa, nso, snk, sun, tgl, ven, xho, zul |
| au | 533 | 20 | bos, glk, hau, kea, msa, oci, pes, run, som, tgl |
| be | 317 | 19 | bos, diq, glg, glk, knn, lin, oci, pes, tha, vls |
| fi | 546 | 35 | ban, bem, bos, kde, knn, ngl, oci, pes, snk, som |
| hu | 131 | 43 | bem, bos, hye, jav, kde, knn, ngl, nya, oci, pes |
| ac.za | 72,867 | 86 | nbl, nso, sot, ssw, tsn, tso, ven, xho, zul |
| eu | 6,355 | 51 | bos, glg, glk, hye, kea, oci, pam, pes, tgl |
| hr | 36,978 | 2,984 | bcl, bos, diq, emk, kde, knn, oci, tgl |
| my | 189,083 | 729 | ban, bcl, jav, min, msa, pes, sun, tgl |
| si | 610 | 146 | bcl, bos, knn, lgg, oci, pes, sus, tha |
| tk | 982 | 36 | bos, glk, kde, kea, mos, msa, nya, pes |
| ws | 1,943 | 24 | bcl, bos, glk, knn, msa, nya, pes, zul |
| ac.jp | 210 | 7 | bcl, glk, hau, khk, kng, nya, tgl |
| at | 722 | 62 | bos, ckb, glk, kea, msa, pes, tgl |
| cl | 62 | 21 | bos, glg, kea, mad, nya, oci, tgl |
| co.jp | 426 | 14 | bem, diq, khk, kng, pes, tgl, zul |
| co.uk | 820,267 | 5 | mkd, msa, nep, nya, pes, run, sqi |
| es | 122,155 | 287 | bos, glg, glk, kea, knn, oci, pes |
| gov | 4,482 | 11 | bcl, hat, kea, pes, som, tgk, tgl |
| gr | 46 | 10 | bos, knn, mos, oci, pag, pes, tha |

Table 4: Most common TLDs with list of languages and their combined amount of sentences and domains.

*Proceedings of the 1st Workshop on Dataset Creation for Lower-Resourced Languages (DCLRL) @LREC2022*, pages 44–52
Marseille, 24 June 2022


# Fine-grained Entailment: Resources for Greek NLI and Precise Entailment

**Eirini Amanaki[*], Jean-Philippe Bernardy[◇], Stergios Chatzikyriakidis[*◇], Robin Cooper[◇], Simon Dobnik[◇], Aram Karimi[◇], Adam Ek[◇], Eirini Chrysovalantou Giannikouri[*], Vasiliki Katsouli[*], Ilias Kolokousis[*], Eirini Chrysovalantou Mamatzaki[*], Dimitrios Papadakis[*], Olga Petrova[*], Erofili Psaltaki[*], Effrosyni Skoulataki[*], Charikleia Soupiona[*], Christina Stefanidou[*]**
[*]Department of Philology, University of Crete
{philp0898}@philology.uoc.gr, {stergios.chatzikyriakidis}@uoc.gr
{philp0899,philp0929,phil5816,philp0900,phil5647,philp0928}@philology.uoc.gr
{philp0883,philp0916,philp0861,philp0862}@philology.uoc.gr
[◇]Centre for Linguistic Theory and Studies in Probability, FLoV, University of Gothenburg
{name.surname}@gu.se

**Abstract**

In this paper, we present a number of fine-grained resources for Natural Language Inference (NLI). In particular, we present a number of resources and validation methods for Greek NLI and a resource for precise NLI. First, we extend the Greek version of the FraCaS test suite to include examples where the inference is directly linked to the syntactic/morphological properties of Greek. The new resource contains an additional 428 examples, making it in total a dataset of 774 examples. Expert annotators have been used in order to create the additional resource, while extensive validation of the original Greek version of the FraCaS by non-expert and expert subjects is performed. Next, we continue the work initiated by (Bernardy and Chatzikyriakidis, 2020), according to which a subset of the RTE problems have been labeled for missing hypotheses and we present a dataset an order of magnitude larger, annotating the whole SuperGlUE/RTE dataset with missing hypotheses. Lastly, we provide a de-dropped version of the Greek XNLI dataset, where the pronouns that are missing due to the pro-drop nature of the language are inserted. We then run some models to see the effect of that insertion and report the results.

**Keywords:** Natural Language Inference, Textual Entailment, FraCaS, RTE, XNLI

## 1. Introduction

Natural Language Inference (NLI, or Textual Entailment, TE) has been a core task in Computational Semantics from its early symbolic years, all the way to the present Deep Learning (DL) era. Indeed, the centrality and importance of NLI has been acknowledged early on by Cooper et al., arguing that NLI is the crux of Computational Semantics, aptly stating that "inferential ability is not only a central manifestation of semantic competence but is in fact centrally constitutive of it" (Cooper et al., 1996). This acknowledgement of the centrality of NLI has continued up to now, with NLI being one of the core tasks for Natural Language Understanding (NLU) and central to NLU benchmarks like GLUE (Vendrov et al., 2016) and SuperGLUE (Wang et al., 2019). To give a further example, one of the most cited papers in NLI (Bowman et al., 2015), argues that understanding inference about entailment and contradiction, in effect the task of NLI, is an important aspect for constructing semantic representations, while on a more practical note, Nie et al. (2020a) note that NLI is arguably the most canonical task in NLU.

Despite the great success in tackling the task of NLI in recent years, questions have started to develop about the efficiency of existing NLI datasets to train good models for NLI. For example, Chatzikyriakidis et al. (2017) have argued that the community should strive for datasets representing data from multiple domains and further include more instances of inference. This plea, as (Poliak, 2020) correctly notes, has been taken into consideration by the community, and indeed a lot of effort has been put in creating more diverse datasets in the last years. Another issue that has arisen w.r.t. dataset development is annotation artifacts, i.e. datasets that contain artifacts due to the way they are constructed, that are leveraged by the models in order to obtain good accuracy. In effect, the models are using low-level heuristics that should not play a role in solving the task. For example, (Poliak et al., 2018) have shown that artefacts and statistical irregularities can help the models perform well on the NLI task, even when only trained on the hypotheses (hypothesis-only). A lot of similar research has verified this: Pham et al. (2020) show that NLI models are not sensitive to word-order, nor to datasets corruption by random POS (part-of-speech) drop (Talman et al., 2021). In contrast, some models seem to be sensitive to changes that should not affect their performance. For example, Glockner et al. (2018) show that the replacement of words with mutually exclusive hyponyms or antonyms hurts performance, while Talman and Chatzikyriakidis (2019) show that models do not generalize well when trained and tested on different NLI datasets.

In this context, the community has tried to come up with responses to these challenges. In terms of dataset creation, a body of research has been arguing for more diverse resources for NLI, as well as the need for datasets that are clean from annotation artefacts. As regards the former, this led to the development of more fine-grained datasets. For example, datasets that test for implicature and presupposition (Jeretic et al., 2020), Numerical/Quantifier reasoning (Kim et al., 2019; Richardson et al., 2019), Monotonicity Reasoning (Yanaka et al., 2019; Richardson et al., 2019), Comparatives, among many others.[1] As regards the latter, work on using adversarial techniques in dataset creation has led in the development of datasets much less prone to annotation artefacts. The Adversarial NLI dataset (Nie et al., 2020b) is an example of such a dataset.

One of the things directly connected to creating diverse NLI datasets, concerns multilingual NLI platforms. There is, of course, the XNLI dataset (Conneau et al., 2018), and also a number of other attempts to produce multilingual datasets for NLI for various languages (Hu et al., 2020; Wijnholds and Moortgat, 2021; Magnini et al., 2014), but in general most of the existing datasets are only in English.

In this paper, we offer a number of fine-grained resources for NLI, two for multilingual NLI, in specific for Greek, and one for precise entailment. More precisely, the paper will report the following work:[2]

- An extension of the Greek version of the FraCaS test suite that includes semantic inferences that are based on idiosyncratic features of Greek syntax. The extension makes the dataset double the size of the original.
- Validation of the original FraCaS test suite for Greek using experts and non-experts against the original annotations and result reporting.
- Completing the work in Bernardy and Chatzikyriakidis (2020) by providing the missing hypotheses (when they exist) for the SuperGLUE RTE dataset. Missing hypotheses refer to information needed to draw an inference, e.g. background knowledge, real-world knowledge, that is however missing in the premises.
- Create a version of the Greek XNLI dataset where all dropped pronouns are inserted, in effect a de-pro-dropped version of Greek. We do this in order to check whether performance of NLI models for Greek is affected if we do so, given that pre-trained language models are trained on English and are subsequently fine-tuned.

# 2. Methods

## 2.1. Extending the Greek FraCaS

The first part of the project involves the extension of the original Greek FraCaS test suite for Greek. What we wanted to achieve is an additional set of inference cases that are dependent on the syntax of Greek. Given that these cases are not so easily found in real-world data, we decided to first use expert constructed changes, focussing on the range of pattern variation for this study. The original Greek FraCaS is a translation of the English FraCaS and has been developed as part of the multi-fracas project at the University of Gothenburg.[3] The additional inference cases added include language dependent syntactic constructions that most of the time do not appear in translations of semantically similar inference cases from English to Greek. To give an example, the additive use of the coordinator *ke* rarely appears in translations of the focus associating operator "too" or "also", but rather appear with the insertion of the element meaning "also" "episis". Other cases include modal discourse markers expressing doubt like "taha" and inferences involving clitic clusters. In more detail, the extra categories added to the suite are as follows:[4]

1. Coordinator ke
    - This involves different uses of the *ke* "and" coordinator in Greek: normal conjunction, both interpretation and additive interpretation among others.
2. Negative Polarity Items
    - Inferences involving a number of negative polarity items in Greek. These include: the semantic negative operator *den* or *min* "not" followed by the NPIs *puthena* "nowhere", *kanenas* "nobody", *tipota* "nothing", *den* followed by *pote* "never" or *kan* "even", and *den* followed by *oute kan* "not even" or *oute* "neither" in embedded sentences. Also, NPIs without a negative operator: *oute kan*, *oudeis* "no one", *kanena* "anything" (existential), and *pouthena - tipota* "nowhere - nothing". There is a section with minimizers, free choice items and PPIs: *mia stalia* "a little", *kati* "something", *opoiondipote* "whoever", *toulaxiston* "at least" and *mono* "just" (Giannakidou (2011)). Lastly, there are inferences with NPIs that mean in dialogues, which highlight idiosyncrasies of Greek because include possible premises of natural speakers such as: *oute kan, pouthena kai tipota* "nothing and nowhere", and *thelondas kai min* "wanting or not".
3. Polydefinites

[1]See (Poliak, 2020) for a complete survey on NLI datasets.

[2]All resources can be found at: `https://github.com/GU-CLASP/LREC_2022/tree/main/datasets`.

[3]`https://gu-clasp.github.io/multifracas/`.

[4]Note that the list of idiosyncratic constructions that are covered in the test suite is not exhaustive. Such an exhaustive list needs further work in order first to decide which these constructions are, followed by creating examples of inference that they are involved.

- Cases that a noun is modified with an adjective and before each phrase the definite article is added (Kolliakou, 2004). While polydefinites can have a variety of semantic uses, we chose only those that have an upward entailment, because those have the most clear-cut reading among speakers.

4. Discourse Markers

   - Inferences involving three different discourse markers in Greek. The discourse markers used are the following: *siga*, *taha* and *ke kala*. *Sigs* is an adverb literally meaning "slowly", but in Greek it is used to express doubt meaning "it is doubtful" and it is associated with negation (Onufrieva, 2019). The word *taha* is an adverb meaning 'supposedly' as does the phrase *ke kala* which literally means "and well".

5. Clitics

   - This involves examples where the inference depends on weak object pronouns, for example cases of clitic clusters, where changing the case marking of the weak object pronoun gives rise to different inference patterns, e.g. the difference between an argumental and an ethical dative interpretation (*mu/me magirepse* "s/he cooked for me/ s/he cooked me").

### 2.2. Validating the FraCaS

The second part of the project involves the validation of the original FraCaS test suite against crowds of experts and non-experts. The validation was performed as a controlled crowd-sourcing data collection task using the Semant-o-matic tool[5] which is used for collection of semantic judgements both by targeting particular groups of participants through advertising experiment locally or on social media (as in traditional experiments and annotation tasks) or reaching out to a larger pool of participants using Amazon Mechanical Turk (Dobnik and Åstbom, 2017; Rajestari et al., 2021). In addition to the task data, questions about the participant background can also be included.

In the current data collection task all examples of the original FraCaS (346) were used. Each was presented as one of more statements (representing premises) and a question corresponding to the conclusion. Participants were instructed to answer the question by only considering information presented in the statements (the purpose was to limit the effect of background knowledge) by choosing one of the three possible answers: "Yes", "No" and "Don't know". The presentation of FraCas examples was randomised for each participant. Each participant was given a chance to provide answers to all 346 examples but there was no requirement to answer all of them as they were allowed to break the task at any time. Note that one can translate this result into a probabilistic version of the FraCaS, if they wished so: the categorical judgements over a set of participants can be translated straightforwardly to probability: the frequency by which annotators make a particular choice is the likelihood that an average annotator would make that choice.

The data was collected from subjects connected with the University of Crete in December 2021 where 175 participants were recruited among students and their social connections. Participants were asked whether they have studied linguistics before. If they answered "yes" they are considered experts (86, 49.14%) and non-experts otherwise (89, 50.86%). In total, they have provided 7,576 judgements which on average makes 21.9 judgements per FraCas example. Experts provided 3,145 judgements (41.51%) while non-experts provided 4,431 judgements (58.49%).

### 2.3. Precise RTE 2.0

The third part of the project involves the continuation of the work by Bernardy and Chatzikyriakidis (2020). There the authors attempt to give a precise platform for textual entailment, by taking a fraction of the RTE platform and annotate them with missing hypotheses.

We have selected all problems from the SuperGLUE/RTE task corpus which were marked as "YES" (i.e. entailment holds). The problems were not further selected nor doctored by us. The problems were then re-rated by masters students in linguistics (in Bernardy and Chatzikyriakidis (2020) experts in linguistics and logic were recruited). For most problems, three subjects were consulted (13 problems were rated by 4 subjects). More precisely, the experts were instructed to reconsider each problem and be especially wary of missing hypotheses, i.e. information used in order to carry out an inference that is however missing in the text. If they considered the entailment to hold, we gave the instruction to optionally mention any additional implicit hypothesis that they would be using. Similarly, if they considered that there was no entailment in the problem, they were suggested to (optionally) give an argument for their judgment — thereby also indirectly indicating missing hypotheses.

### 2.4. De-dropped XNLI

In the fourth part of the project, we investigate the effect of pro-drop in the performance of NLI models. For this reason we developed the augmented dataset depro-XNLI, where all the Greek examples have been changed by inserting all the pronouns that are missing, given the pro-drop nature of the language. We took the English cases as the basis, and inserted all pronouns that are present in English, but not in the Greek translation (see Table 1). A note on terminology here: we will be using the words de-drop/de-dropped for the pro-

[5] http://www.dobnik.net/simon/semant-o-matic/

cess/result of making a pro-drop language non pro-drop by inserting the missing pronouns.

| | Premise | Hypothesis |
|---|---|---|
| English | *I think that's why I remember that.* | *I didn't remember it at all.* |
| Greek | *Νομίζω αυτός είναι ο λόγος που το θυμάμαι αυτό* | *Δεν το θυμήθηκα καθόλου* |
| Greek de-drop | **ΕΓΩ** νομίζω αυτός είναι ο λόγος που το θυμάμαι αυτό | ***ΕΓΩ*** *δεν το θυ μήθηκα καθόλου* |

Table 1: First row: Original English pairs. Second row: Translation to Greek as found in XNLI. Third row: pronoun insertion

## 3. Results and Analyses

### 3.1. Extended Greek FraCaS (EX-GR-FraCaS)

The new extended FraCaS dataset for Greek includes 774 examples of inference and can be seen as including two main parts: the existing original part[6], which is the translation of the original English FraCaS test suite into Greek and the second part, our addition, which includes a total of 428 further examples of inference that involve idiosyncratic features of Greek syntax according to the categories as these are specified in 2.1..[7] Furthermore, the original FraCaS test suite is highly imbalanced between the three categories. One can clearly see that from 3.1., where there is a clear dominance of YES examples, which take more than half the suite, approximately 0.27% are NO examples, and UNK examples are very few, comprising approximately 0.09% of the suite. Note that the original FraCaS has an additional category created by MacCartney and Manning (2007) in order to deal with defective examples that were either missing the hypothesis, or examples that had non-standard answers (e.g. Yes, on one reading) etc. This is not a negligible part of the suite as it comprises approximately 12% of the suite. The extension of the dataset is much more balanced w.r.t the three inference categories, with the YES examples comprising approximately 35% of the dataset, NO examples approximately 31%, and UNK examples approximately 34%. There are no undefined examples. The results are shown in 3.1.. Three examples from the new dataset are shown below. One involves *kanenas* "nobody", the other one *taxa* "supposedly" and the last one has to do with *kai* "and":

(1) A Yes example from the EX-GR-FraCaS test suite.

**P1** Δεν ήρθε κανένας στη σημερινή παράσταση.
Nobody came at today's performance.

**P2** Μόνο ο Γιώργος.
Just Giorgos.

**Q.** Ήρθε ο Γιώργος στη σημερινή παράσταση;
Did Giorgos come the today's performance?

**H.** Ο Γιώργος ήρθε στη σημερινή παράσταση.
Giorgos came at the today's performance.

**Label** Ναι.
Yes.

(2) An No example from the EX-GR-FraCaS test suite.

**P** Κοιτούσε συνέχεια το κινητό του, δεν τηλεφώνησε καν η μαμά του.
He kept looking at his phone, even his mom didn't call.

**Q.** Είναι αληθές, ότι η μαμά δεν τον καλεί συνήθως;
Is it true, that mom does not usually call him?

**H.** Η μαμά δεν τον καλεί συνήθως
Mom does not usually call him.

**Label** Όχι.
No.

(3) An UNK example from the EX-GR-FraCaS test suite.

**P** Ο Γιώργος τάχα μου τους έβλεπε πρώτη φορά στη ζωή του.
Giorgos supposedly saw them for the first time.

**Q.** Ο Γιώργος τους έβλεπε πρώτη φορά στη ζωή του;
Did Giorgos see them for the first time ever?

**H.** Ο Γιώργος τους έβλεπε πρώτη φορά στη ζωή του.
Giorgos saw them for the first time ever.

**Label** Δεν ξέρω.
I don't know.

### 3.2. Validation of the FraCaS

Figure 1 shows the results of the FraCaS validation by human judges (see Section 2.2.). The aim of the eval-

[6] https://github.com/GU-CLASP/multifracas/blob/master/fracas_greek_final_ipa_team_crete.xml.

[7] https://gu-clasp.github.io/multifracas/fracas_greek_extended_team_crete.xml

| | FraCaS (original) | Addendum | EFraCaS |
|---|---|---|---|
| E | 180 | 153 | 333 |
| C | 94 | 130 | 224 |
| UNK | 31 | 145 | 176 |
| UND | 41 | 0 | 41 |
| TOTAL | 346 | 428 | 774 |

Table 2: E stands for Entailment problems, C for Contradiction problems, UNK for neutral problems and UND for undefined. The Addendum are the extra examples added to the original Greek FraCaS, and EFraCaS the concatenation of the original Greek FraCaS and the Addendum.

uation is to examine distribution of judgments for different FraCaS categories and whether the distributions are affected by the bias from being familiar with the task. Natural language examples allow different interpretation of premises and conclusions leading to different judgments of inference, for example due to lexical ambiguity of words. This is most clearly expressed in the category "undefined". There may also be a difference in the way experts and non-experts understand inference in natural language. The horizontal axis shows the answer provided in the dataset by their designers and the vertical axis shows a percentage bar of the answers provided by human judges. For each FraCaS label we provide three bars which represent (i) all answers, (ii) expert answers, and (iii) non-expert answers. Note again that the original FraCas is imbalanced in the distribution of ground-truth labels. Out of 346 examples, there 203 (58.67%) "yes" answers, 33 (9.54%) "no" answers, 98 (28.32%) "unknown" answers and 12 (3.47%) "undef" answers. The undefined answers are difficult cases for which it was not possible to assign a different label unambiguously.

Overall there is a strong agreement with the FraCas score on "yes" and "no" classes. Sometimes examples of the yes and no classes are labelled as "unknown" and "no", possibly because participants might be bringing in additional background knowledge to resolve inference. The reason for this might be lexical or structural ambiguity of individual examples. For the examples labelled as "unknown" there is a participant bias to provide either a "yes" or "no" answer. Interestingly, this bias is lower with the "undef" label, thus those those cases that allow alternative interpretations.

A comparison of answers provided by participants who self-reported to have studied linguistics (second column) versus those who have not (third column) reveals that there are no differences between them. A $\chi^2$ test finds no significant difference between "yes" ($p = 0.3791$), "no" ($p = .1508$), "unknown" ($p = 0.2573$) and "undef" ($p = 0.8590$) answers of linguists and non-linguists. This indicates that prior linguistic training does not have a bias on the performance on this general inference task for which no linguistic training is required. Note that the status of linguistic expertise is self reported and that participants answering this question with "yes" might have had different backgrounds and degrees of linguistic training.

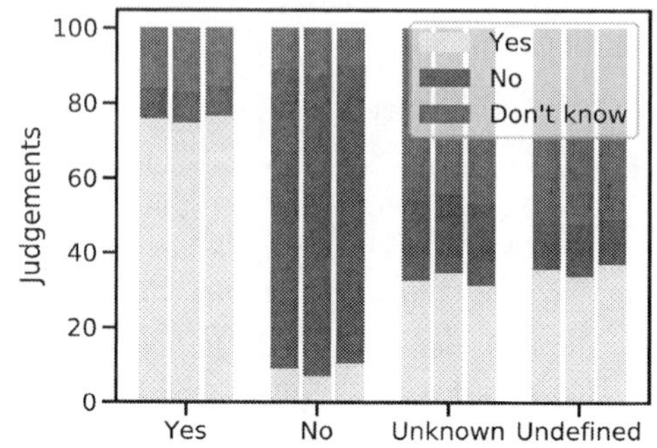


(a) all judgements

Figure 1: Results of the FraCaS validation through crowd-sourcing. Each FraCaS label on the horizontal axis is associated with three bars which represent (i) all answers, (ii) expert answers, and (iii) non-expert answers.

### 3.3. Precise RTE 2.0

In the process, we have gathered a total of 3760 judgments, 593 missing hypotheses and 331 explanations for negative judgments. The entailment judgments are found in Fig. 2.

Despite all original problems being classified as "yes" by the creators of the RTE test suite — we find here that on average, one subject in 5 is likely to cast a doubt over this "yes". Here, we count as a doubt either a response of "no" or "yes" with missing hypotheses.

**"Yes if ..." vs "No because ..."?** We elected to group those categories in our summaries, because the classification between "yes" with missing hypotheses and "no" is a tenuous one. Indeed, experts often find the same missing hypotheses but classify the problems differently (as "yes" or "no").

We find that missing hyphotheses tend not to be discovered by all subjects. As evidence, the agreement factor (Fleiss' Kappa) when grouping answers in the doubtful/certain categories is $\kappa$=0.16.

Another way to look at the data is to count the number of experts casting doubt on an entailment problem. In Fig. 3, we show the distribution of number of experts casting doubt on entailment, over all problems, as a histogram.

To sum up,

1. Perfect agreement (0 or 3 doubts) occur in 47 percent of cases.

2. The probability of having a three doubts being cast is the lowest.

| Type | Count | Ratio |
|---|---|---|
| Yes, with no missing hypothesis | 2636 | 0.70 |
| Yes, with missing hypotheses | 593 | 0.16 |
| No, with no explanation | 200 | 0.05 |
| No, with explanation | 331 | 0.09 |
| Total of doubtful entailment | 734 | 0.20 |
| Total of any type | 3760 | 1 |

Figure 2: Number of responses by type

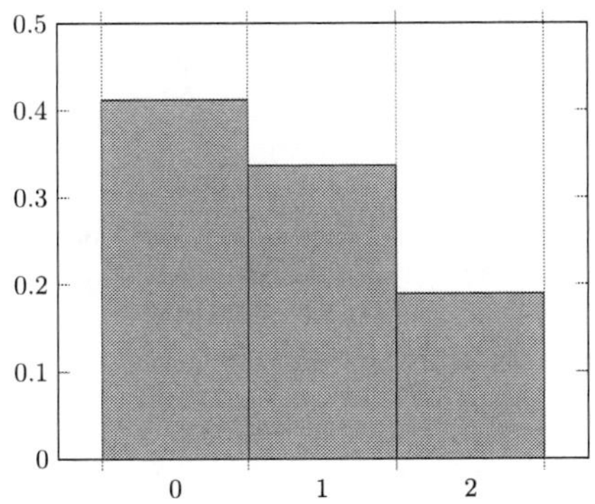


Figure 3: Distribution of the number of doubtful subjects.

We find this level of agreement indicative of a good level of reliability. Additionally, with three experts per problem, we are likely to discover most missing hypotheses and incorrect entailments.

In this setting, we have found that subjects were less likely to cast doubt on entailment than Bernardy and Chatzikyriakidis (2020). We conjecture that this is because master students are less likely to discover gaps in reasoning than the more seasoned experts (PhD or professors in linguistics or logic) consulted by Bernardy and Chatzikyriakidis (2020). The size of the sample might also have an effect, given that it is ten times the size of the original. It would be interesting to repeat the experiment with more seasoned experts or the other way around, i.e. use the smaller sample with less experienced annotators. In any case, the other issue that this discrepancy between the number of missing premises identified in Bernardy and Chatzikyriakidis (2020) and the smaller number we have found in this study shows, is that the task of finding missing premises is rather open-ended and can go to different levels of fine-grainedness. This further shows the problem with some cases of inference, namely that a lot of missing knowledge has to be recognized by the model and/or find a way to make the inference in a way that resembles this kind of reasoning under hidden premises.

### 3.4. De-dropped XNLI

We evaluate the effect of inserting pronouns in the Greek XNLI dataset to investigate whether the pro-drop differences of the languages have an effect in the performance of the models. Our goal here is to not to make other languages similar to English, but to investigate the importance of pro-drop in such tasks, if any. We use the XLM-RoBERTa (Conneau et al., 2019) model trained on the English MNLI dataset (Williams et al., 2017). Our model uses max-pooling over the word representations to obtain a sentence representation. We found this method more effective than taking the CLS representation. In the experiment we evaluate how effective transfer learning is when presented with unusual syntax (that does not alter the meaning) in Table 3.

| Data | Accuracy |
|---|---|
| Original | 75.0 |
| De-drop | 74.8 |

Table 3: Results on the original XNLI data and the de-dropped data.

The results show a small drop in accuracy of 0.2 percentage points. This indicates that for models trained on English NLI examples, when transferring the knowledge to Greek, models are able to account for examples where dropped pronouns have been added back to the sentence. However, as can be seen in Table 1, adding the pronouns may result in a lexical overlap between the premise and hypothesis which the model can exploit. For this reason, we also test the scenario where only the premise or the hypothesis have the inserted pronouns in Table 4.

| Premise | Hypothesis | Accuracy |
|---|---|---|
| Original | De-drop | 68.8 |
| De-drop | Original | 68.9 |

Table 4: Results when de-dropping either the premise or hypothesis.

When only one of either the premise or hypothesis have the pronoun inserted we see that the performance degrades by 6.2 percentage points. This indicates that while some cases of inserted pronouns are handled correctly by the model, it also changes the label on some examples. In addition to highlighting issues NLI models have with inserting pronouns, this also shows that the models also rely on the lexical overlap between the premise and hypothesis, even when the overlap is non-consequential pronouns.

## 4. Conclusion and Future Work

In this paper, we provided a number of resources for Greek NLI, as well as precise entailment. More specifically, we extended the FraCaS test suite for Greek to further include cases of inference that are dependent on language specific syntax. The resulting test suite is double the size of the original one. We believe that such an extension can be taken as a starting point for developing multilingual NLI datasets that cover the wealth of reasoning patterns in interaction with language dependent syntax.

Next, we performed a validation of the original FraCaS test suite for Greek against both experts and non-experts. The results show a number of good agreement with the original test suite, even though some digressions exist, especially for the UNK category. No significant difference between expert and non-expert annotation has been found.

Connected to the previous is the finding that cases of entailment in datasets like the RTE involve hidden premises that are implicitly taken into consideration in the inference process. Following the work by Bernardy and Chatzikyriakidis (2020), we provided annotation of these missing premises for the whole RTE as this is found in SuperGLUE.

Lastly, we presented a variation of the XNLI Greek dataset, where all pronouns included in the original English examples and are missing in the Greek version, due to the pro-drop nature of the language, are introduced. This leads to the creation of a de-dropped XNLI dataset for Greek. We wanted to test the hypothesis of whether this data augmentation/corruption will have an effect on model performance. No effect was found when the new de-dropped dataset was used. However, an effect was found when we used a hybrid format: a) the premises are in the original format but the hypotheses in the de-dropped form and b) vice versa. In these cases, we found a significant drop in performance which points to the system exploiting various lexical overlap cues in deciding inference.

We believe that what we have proposed in this paper can be extended to multiple languages, but also to multiple task investigations. As regards the former, we believe that the idea of providing examples of inference based on idiosyncratic syntax of the target languages is a promising way towards better multilingual NLI and we hope that more researchers will pick up on this idea. The next step is to ground these new example cases in natural data. This is what we plan to do in future work. The results in the validation task, as well as the annotation for missing inferences brings out the fact that inference is not one consistent thing, but rather varies depending on context, expertise, domain and so on. It also brings out the fact that the annotation guidelines are extremely crucial in the results one gets w.r.t inference. One promising way to further extend this work is to design systems that can automatically infer hidden premises given a premise, a hypothesis and their label. Lastly, w.r.t the last part of the paper, where a de-dropped version of the Greek XNLI dataset was presented, such a dataset or similar dataset can investigate more theoretical issues w.r.t to various linguistic features that vary between languages, pro-drop being one of them. This will eventually lead in NLP working closer with Theoretical Linguistics in order to investigate theoretical claims made w.r.t these varying features.

## 5. Ethical Considerations and Broader Impact

There are no ethical considerations in the work described in this paper. No handling of personal or any other kind of sensitive information has been done and no models that have a considerate carbon footprint for to their training have been used.
As regards the broader impact of this work, we aspire to help in the democratization of NLP by creating resources for lesser, in terms of data, languages. We hope that such endeavours for creating datasets for low-rerource languages will intensify in the future.

## 6. Acknowledgements

Jean-Philippe Bernardy, Stergios Chatzikyriakidis, Robin Cooper, Simon Dobnik, Adam Ek and Aram Karimi are supported by grant 2014-39 from the Swedish Research Council, which funds the Centre for Linguistic Theory and Studies in Probability (CLASP) in the Department of Philosophy, Linguistics, and Theory of Science at the University of Gothenburg.

Bernardy, J.-P. and Chatzikyriakidis, S. (2020). Improving the precision of natural textual entailment problem datasets. In Proceedings of the 12th Language Resources and Evaluation Conference, pages 6835–6840.

Bowman, S. R., Angeli, G., Potts, C., and Manning, C. D. (2015). A large annotated corpus for learning natural language inference. In Lluís Màrquez, et al., editors, Proceedings of the 2015 Conference on Empirical Methods in Natural Language Processing, EMNLP 2015, Lisbon, Portugal, September 17-21, 2015, pages 632–642. The Association for Computational Linguistics.

Chatzikyriakidis, S., Cooper, R., Dobnik, S., and Larsson, S. (2017). An overview of natural language inference data collection: The way forward? In Proceedings of the Computing Natural Language Inference Workshop.

Conneau, A., Rinott, R., Lample, G., Williams, A., Bowman, S., Schwenk, H., and Stoyanov, V. (2018). Xnli: Evaluating cross-lingual sentence representations. In Proceedings of the 2018 Conference on Empirical Methods in Natural Language Processing, pages 2475–2485.

Conneau, A., Khandelwal, K., Goyal, N., Chaudhary, V., Wenzek, G., Guzmán, F., Grave, E., Ott, M., Zettlemoyer, L., and Stoyanov, V. (2019). Unsupervised cross-lingual representation learning at scale. arXiv preprint arXiv:1911.02116.

Cooper, R., Crouch, D., Van Eijck, J., Fox, C., Van Genabith, J., Jaspars, J., Kamp, H., Milward, D., Pinkal, M., Poesio, M., et al. (1996). Using the framework. Technical report.

Dobnik, S. and Åstbom, A. (2017). (Perceptual) grounding as interaction. In Volha Petukhova et al., editors, Proceedings of Saardial – Semdial 2017: The

21st Workshop on the Semantics and Pragmatics of Dialogue, pages 17–26, Saarbrücken, Germany, August 15–17.

Giannakidou, A. (2011). Negative and positive polarity items. De Gruyter Mouton, 2:1660–1712.

Glockner, M., Shwartz, V., and Goldberg, Y. (2018). Breaking nli systems with sentences that require simple lexical inferences. In The 56th Annual Meeting of the Association for Computational Linguistics (ACL), Melbourne, Australia, July.

Hu, H., Richardson, K., Xu, L., Li, L., Kübler, S., and Moss, L. S. (2020). Ocnli: Original chinese natural language inference. In Proceedings of the 2020 Conference on Empirical Methods in Natural Language Processing: Findings, pages 3512–3526.

Jeretic, P., Warstadt, A., Bhooshan, S., and Williams, A. (2020). Are natural language inference models imppressive? learning implicature and presupposition. In Proceedings of the 58th Annual Meeting of the Association for Computational Linguistics, pages 8690–8705.

Kim, N., Patel, R., Poliak, A., Xia, P., Wang, A., McCoy, T., Tenney, I., Ross, A., Linzen, T., Van Durme, B., et al. (2019). Probing what different nlp tasks teach machines about function word comprehension. In Proceedings of the Eighth Joint Conference on Lexical and Computational Semantics (* SEM 2019), pages 235–249.

Kolliakou, D. (2004). Monadic definites and polydefinites: their form, meaning and use. Journal of linguistics, 40(2):263–323.

MacCartney, B. and Manning, C. D. (2007). Natural logic for textual inference. In Proceedings of the ACL-PASCAL Workshop on Textual Entailment and Paraphrasing, pages 193–200. Association for Computational Linguistics.

Magnini, B., Zanoli, R., Dagan, I., Eichler, K., Neumann, G., Noh, T.-G., Pado, S., Stern, A., and Levy, O. (2014). The excitement open platform for textual inferences. In Proceedings of 52nd annual meeting of the association for computational linguistics: system demonstrations, pages 43–48.

Nie, Y., Williams, A., Dinan, E., Bansal, M., Weston, J., and Kiela, D. (2020a). Adversarial NLI: A new benchmark for natural language understanding. In Dan Jurafsky, et al., editors, Proceedings of the 58th Annual Meeting of the Association for Computational Linguistics, ACL 2020, Online, July 5-10, 2020, pages 4885–4901. Association for Computational Linguistics.

Nie, Y., Williams, A., Dinan, E., Bansal, M., Weston, J., and Kiela, D. (2020b). Adversarial nli: A new benchmark for natural language understanding. In Proceedings of the 58th Annual Meeting of the Association for Computational Linguistics, pages 4885–4901.

Onufrieva, E. (2019). Συντακτικοί φρασεολογισμοί με σημασία άρνησης στη νέα ελληνική. In Μελέτες για την ελληνική γλώσσα 39, pages 1143–1158.

Pham, T. M., Bui, T., Mai, L., and Nguyen, A. (2020). Out of order: How important is the sequential order of words in a sentence in natural language understanding tasks? arXiv preprint arXiv:2012.15180.

Poliak, A., Naradowsky, J., Haldar, A., Rudinger, R., and Van Durme, B. (2018). Hypothesis only baselines in natural language inference. In Proceedings of the Seventh Joint Conference on Lexical and Computational Semantics, pages 180–191. Association for Computational Linguistics.

Poliak, A. (2020). A survey on recognizing textual entailment as an nlp evaluation. arXiv preprint arXiv:2010.03061.

Rajestari, M., Dobnik, S., Cooper, R., and Karimi, A. (2021). Very necessary: the meaning of non-gradable modal adjectives in discourse contexts. In Peter Ljunglöf, et al., editors, Selected contributions from the Eighth Swedish Lan- guage Technology Conference (SLTC-2020), volume 184 of NEALT Proceedings Series, No. XX, Gothenburg, Sweden, 25–27 November. Northern European Association for Language Technology (NEALT), Linköping University Electronic Press: Linköping Electronic Conference Proceedings.

Richardson, K., Hu, H., Moss, L. S., and Sabharwal, A. (2019). Probing natural language inference models through semantic fragments. CoRR, abs/1909.07521.

Talman, A. and Chatzikyriakidis, S. (2019). Testing the generalization power of neural network models across NLI benchmarks. In Proceedings of the 2019 ACL Workshop BlackboxNLP: Analyzing and Interpreting Neural Networks for NLP, pages 85–94, Florence, Italy, August. Association for Computational Linguistics.

Talman, A., Apidianaki, M., Chatzikyriakidis, S., and Tiedemann, J. (2021). NLI data sanity check: Assessing the effect of data corruption on model performance. In Proceedings of the 23rd Nordic Conference on Computational Linguistics (NoDaLiDa), pages 276–287, Reykjavik, Iceland (Online), May 31–2 June. Linköping University Electronic Press, Sweden.

Vendrov, I., Kiros, R., Fidler, S., and Urtasun, R. (2016). Order-embeddings of images and language. In Yoshua Bengio et al., editors, 4th International Conference on Learning Representations, ICLR 2016, San Juan, Puerto Rico, May 2-4, 2016, Conference Track Proceedings.

Wang, A., Pruksachatkun, Y., Nangia, N., Singh, A., Michael, J., Hill, F., Levy, O., and Bowman, S. (2019). Superglue: A stickier benchmark for general-purpose language understanding systems. In Advances in Neural Information Processing Systems, pages 3266–3280.

Wijnholds, G. and Moortgat, M. (2021). Sicknl: A dataset for dutch natural language inference. In Proceedings of the 16th Conference of the European Chapter of the Association for Computational Linguistics: Main Volume, pages 1474–1479.

Williams, A., Nangia, N., and Bowman, S. R. (2017). A broad-coverage challenge corpus for sentence understanding through inference. arXiv preprint arXiv:1704.05426.

Yanaka, H., Mineshima, K., Bekki, D., Inui, K., Sekine, S., Abzianidze, L., and Bos, J. (2019). Can neural networks understand monotonicity reasoning? In Proceedings of the 2019 ACL Workshop BlackboxNLP: Analyzing and Interpreting Neural Networks for NLP, pages 31–40.

*Proceedings of the 1st Workshop on Dataset Creation for Lower-Resourced Languages (DCLRL) @LREC2022*, pages 53–62
Marseille, 24 June 2022


# *Words.hk*: a Comprehensive Cantonese Dictionary Dataset with Definitions, Translations and Transliterated Examples

**Chaak Ming Lau*, Grace Wing-yan Chan***
**Raymond Ka-wai Tse†, Lilian Suet-ying Chan‡**
*The Education University of Hong Kong, 10 Lo Ping Road, Tai Po, Hong Kong
†The Hong Kong University of Science and Technology, Clear Water Bay, Kowloon, Hong Kong
‡Words.hk
{lchaakming, cwyan}@eduhk.hk, kwtseab@connect.ust.hk, info@words.hk

**Abstract**

This paper discusses the compilation of the *words.hk* Cantonese dictionary dataset, which was compiled through manual annotation over a period of 7 years. Cantonese is a low-resource language with limited tagged or manually checked resources, especially at the sentential level, and this dataset is an attempt to fill the gap. The dataset contains over 53,000 entries of Cantonese words, which comes with basic lexical information (Jyutping phonemic transcription, part-of-speech tags, usage tags), manually crafted definitions in Written Cantonese, English translations, and Cantonese examples with English translation and Jyutping transliterations. Special attention has been paid to handle character variants, so that unintended "character errors"(equivalent to typos in phonemic writing systems) are filtered out, and intra-speaker variants are handled. Fine details on word segmentation, character variant handling, definition crafting will be discussed. The dataset can be used in a wide range of natural language processing tasks, such as word segmentation, construction of semantic web and training of models for Cantonese transliteration.

**Keywords:** Cantonese dictionary, diglossia, corpora, Jyutping, parts of speech, word segmentation, character variants, semantic web, crowdsourcing

## 1. Introduction

This paper discusses the compilation and properties of a Cantonese dictionary dataset which includes basic lexical information, Cantonese and English definitions and transliterated examples.

Cantonese (ISO-639-3: yue) is a linguistic variety spoken in Hong Kong, Macau, Guangzhou, and several cities or towns with Cantonese immigrants over the past centuries. As a member of Yue dialect group of the Sinitic language(s), Cantonese serves as the lingua franca of Hong Kong in both formal and informal settings across the city (Lai, 2013; Bacon-Shone et al., 2015), and is used as one of the medium of instruction in the formal education system.

Cantonese will be of interest to the language resource community due to its status a low-resource language and at the same time the most resourceful non-Mandarin Chinese language. Cantonese is often considered a dialect in the education system despite its dominant usage, and falls under a diglossic division of labor with a localized version of Standard Written Chinese (SWC). The implication of this diglossic situation is that most written resources, including transcripts are customarily translated into SWC by the user at the time of writing, making it extremely difficult to obtain Cantonese data. On the other hand, the spoken language has a huge user base and numerous video resources, making it a good starting point to explore resource development for a non-Mandarin Chinese language. Language resource work done for Cantonese has the potential to be transferred to other nearby Chinese linguistic varieties (e.g. Hakka, Teochew, Shanghainese, etc.).

There is a need to obtain not just naturally occurring text from Hong Kong users of Cantonese, for those texts will be a mixture of SWC and Cantonese. The fact that Cantonese is not standardized (although the spoken form was "codified" by the mass media, with a relatively stable phonology and grammar) can partially account for the lack of unmixed Cantonese resources. The paper presents the compilation of a resource that is in "authentic" Written Cantonese (Snow, 2004) that is a faithful representation of the lexical and grammatical aspects of the spoken language.

### 1.1. Existing Resources

At the time of writing Cantonese remains to be a low-resource language due to the factors discussed above. Lexicons and corpora are available for the language, yet are still relatively scarce when compared to languages with similar populations like Korean, Italian, or Polish.

Lexicons with basic lexical information (*Cifu*, *Rime-Cantonese*, *CyberCan*) are readily available but there are not enough resources at higher linguistic levels, partly due to licensing issues. There is a lack of high quality corpus resources (*HKCanCor* and *CantoMap* are the only available open-access corpora), which makes it difficult to compile

| Name | Type | Size | License |
|---|---|---|---|
| *Cifu* (Lai and Winterstein, 2020) | Lexicon | 51,798 words | GPLv3 |
| *Rime-Cantonese* | Lexicon (Input Method) | 185,809 items | CC-BY-4.0 |
| *CyberCan* (Shen et al., 2021) | Lexicon | 133,212 words | CC-BY-4.0 |
| *Cantonese WordNet* (Sio and da Costa, 2019) | Wordnet | 3,500 concepts, 12,000 senses | CC-BY-4.0 |
| *HKCanCor* (Luke and Wong, 2015) | Corpus | 230,000 words | CC-BY-4.0 |
| *CantoMap* (Winterstein et al., 2020) | Corpus | 105,000 words | GPLv3 |
| *HKCAC* (Leung and Law, 2001) | Corpus | 170,000 words | Proprietary |
| *ABC Cantonese-English Comprehensive Dictionary* (Bauer, 2020) | Dictionary | 15,000 entries | Proprietary |
| *CC-Canto* | Dictionary | 34,335 words | CC-BY-SA-3.0 |
| *CantoDict* | Dictionary | 60,714 words | Proprietary |

Table 1: Selected Cantonese language resources

larger-scale semantic webs or dictionaries.

### 1.2. The Project

The submitted dataset is a resource developed by the Cantonese dictionary project 粵典 (*words.hk*), founded in 2014 by the first author and a couple of associates (Lau, 2019). It is the only dictionary of comparable scale that contains detailed explanations of Cantonese words in both Cantonese and English, acting as both a monolingual and bilingual dictionary. As of writing, the project contains more than 53,000 dictionary entries, of which more than 11,550 have been thoroughly reviewed and made available to the general public. Other entries are available for research purposes.

The following section explains the compilation process (section 2), the philosophy of word segmentation and entry creation (section 3), linguistic considerations (sections 4, 5, 6), the crafting of new entries (section 7), data format (section 8), licensing issues (section 9) and future work (section 10).

## 2. Compilation Process

Creating a comprehensive, monolingual dictionary from scratch is a non-trivial task. We adopted a multipronged approach in constructing the dictionary.

### 2.1. Initial Data

We started with word lists from previous projects, for example a list from an unpublished dictionary prepared by the Department of Linguistics of the University of Hong Kong, Hong Kong Education Bureau *Lexical Items with English Explanations for Fundamental Chinese Learning in Hong Kong Schools* (which contains basic words that learners of SWC are expected to know), and the Dictionary of Cantonese Slang (Hutton and Bolton, 2005), as the initial foundation of *words.hk*. Some data from MoeDict[1] were also imported for editor's reference for words that are shared among SWC and Cantonese.

### 2.2. Crowd-editing

*Words.hk* was designed to be a crowd-editing project from the onset, and it fits the description of a crowd-sourcing project summarized by Estellés-Arolas and González-Ladrón-de Guevara (2012): it has a clearly defined goal, participative in nature and internet-based. A wiki-like online system was deployed in 2014 for registered users, most of them volunteers recruited from social media, to contribute to the project.

Since then, about 300 people have made at least one edit, and, as of today, around 20 editors contribute regularly. The cumulative number of revisions made to all dictionary entries totals 150,000. Other than editing existing entries, editors are also granted the right (and encouraged) to create new ones. While no structured process is implemented to tease out new entries, editors are keen to create entries for words they consider sufficiently significant. The search result interface would also prompt editors to create a new entry if the word could not be found in the dictionary. These editor-initiated entries often reflect their diverse background and lived experiences, providing the dictionary with a rich variety of entries, ranging from

[1]MoeDict (萌典), which stands for the Ministry of Education Dictionary, is an online dictionary developed by the open source community in Taiwan.

slangs used by local blue-collar workers, to specialized terms used in medical and scientific fields. This organic process allows the project to capture words that would often be passed over by a dictionary produced in a strictly academic setting that relies on written records.

New editors are trained under an informal system akin to apprenticeship. New editors typically start off with editing existing entries; their first few edits will be reviewed by a more senior editor and feedback would be given. Editors usually gravitate towards working on aspects they felt capable of; some editors focus on Cantonese definitions, some focus on English translations, some on Jyutping romanisation while some other on examples. A specialization system is naturally formed, thereby assuring most of the entries are crafted and cross-checked by multiple editors.

Prior to the ongoing COVID-19 pandemic, we also organized meetups on a regular basis. Editors (especially new ones) were invited to attend and would be assigned to work on particular items (e.g. idiomatic expressions) in small groups. Besides induction of new editors, the meetups allowed editors to discuss issues face to face, complementing the existing online channels. With these activities and communication channels, cohesion, mutual understanding and shared responsibility could be maintained among our team members.

In some years, we also hired university students as summer interns to work on the dictionary. Working under direct supervision of the chief editor, the interns served as a cadre to spearhead specific tasks and set the example for fellow editors with their high standard of work. Many of the interns have continued to contribute to *words.hk* well after the end of their contract, eventually becoming an integral part of the community.[2]

### 2.3. Web-scraping

The relatively small volume of available Cantonese corpora led us to abandon data driven methods in favor of a more manual approach initially, since most NLP techniques applied to Cantonese have been largely ineffective in helping us achieve our goals. For instance, due to diglossia and the small size of existing corpora, frequency data was not a good indicator for entry prioritization.

That said, we recently started inspecting high frequency bigrams and trigrams compiled from data crawled from Hong Kong online forums, resulting in about 1,000 new entries to our word list. This is labor-intensive work as predicted, since most words had already been included in our existing dataset. Editors must sift through false positives of word combinations (e.g. 屋企喺 *uk1kei2 hai2*, "home is at"), typographic errors and proper names (celebrities or user handles).

[2]The third author was an intern in our early years. He is now the chief editor.

### 2.4. Quality Control

We employed technology when applicable to facilitate our workflows. To reduce personal bias and facilitate crowdsourcing, we adopted multiple interaction approaches. When editing and cross-checking entries, editors can leave comments in the column for internal reference. Editing histories are also preserved and made visible to all editors for record-keeping. In addition, public users can report issues on a form on our website or by email.

To ensure correctness in our published entries, all new entries are unpublished when created, and only a handful of senior editors have the rights to publish an entry. In practice the chief editor publishes the vast majority of entries. The chief editor is assisted by a review system where any editor can mark an entry as reviewed. This gives the chief editor an additional assurance vouching for the accuracy of the entry, and allows the system to prioritize entries that have already been reviewed by others for the chief editor's final review before publication.

## 3. Segmentation

In earlier Cantonese dictionary or corpus projects, significant time was put into deciding what should and what should not be listed as an entry. It is probably impossible to come up with a wordhood test that is universally accepted by linguists. Sproat et al. (1996) showed that Chinese speakers do not have a consensus on where the word boundaries lie, whereas inter-subject agreement on word segmentation was around 70% prior to training. A similar issue is found in the handling of Cantonese data.

The primary consideration here is whether segmentation will affect lexicographic functions (Bergenholtz and Tarp, 2003). This wordhood issue does not constitute a problem as long as we allow multiple ways to segment a string into words. For instance, 女朋友 (*neoi5pang4jau5*, "girlfriend") can be listed as one entry, and the constituents 女 (*neoi5*, "female") and 朋友 (*pang4jau5*, "friend") will be listed as separate entries. The second part is further divided into 朋 and 友, and recorded as separate morphemes in the dataset. This treatment creates some redundancies in the entries, but avoids the need to make difficult decisions about removal or non-removal of entries, which is essential to foster growth of the dictionary as a crowdsourcing project. Important collocations are included, on the same ground. 打 (*daa2*) is literally "to hit" but it is also semantically vacuous when used in conjunction with 官司 (*gun1si1*, "lawsuit"), 比賽 (*bei2coi3*, "match"), 電話 (*din6waa2*,

"phone"). These collocations are listed as separate entries despite their phrasal nature. The same morpheme may be split into multiple entries (if it is used in more than one parts-of-speech). Expressions which can be broken down into smaller units will be included if the inclusion of the entry will benefit the learners or other downstream processing tasks.
The dataset is not meant to be a reliable way to measure the size of the Cantonese vocabulary, and the only drawback is slightly higher maintenance cost due to more entries.

## 4. Orthographic Representation

*Words.hk* aims to record Cantonese data as used in Hong Kong, which means the Traditional Chinese script (ISO 15924: *Hant*) is the natural choice for the entries and the definitions. We do not insist on having all morphemes assigned a Traditional Chinese character due to impracticality. There is a fair amount of code-mixing in Cantonese speech of speakers at all education levels. The project maintains a pragmatic approach and includes all words of enough significance regardless of etymology. English loanwords are represented as is (or in a localized form) in the Latin alphabet to faithfully represent how Cantonese words are written. Other Cantonese words that are traditionally represented using letters include compounds of a mixed etymology, onomatopoeic words and native words with obscure origins.

### 4.1. Character Choice

The treatment of language resources for a language without explicit standardization is a matter that calls for thorough documentation. The descriptive nature of the dictionary does not mean that all unconventional written forms will be recorded. In fact, using a purely frequency-based account will rule out well-justified orthographic forms and include a long list of forms that are considered incorrect by most users. The project is descriptive to the level that we try to describe the preferred or perceived-to-be-correct forms (if they exist) of educated users of the language.
The principles we follow include:

1. If a word is of Classical Chinese origin or it is shared with SWC, and there is no dispute in their standardized form as used in Hong Kong, this form will be used.

2. If a word is of English origin, the Standard English spelling (British) will be used.

3. If a word is a native Cantonese word with unsettled etymological dispute, or is onomatopoeic which does not have a conventional written form, forms listed in other paper-based dictionaries and/or attested forms will be included at the discretion of the editorial team.

4. If there are no available Han characters or conventional English spellings for the morpheme, its Jyutping spelling (with the tone numbers removed) will be used as its default representation.

### 4.2. The Equivalent of "Misspelling" in Cantonese

Online Written Cantonese data is known to contain incorrect (as judged by the majority of native speakers) characters, due to the spontaneous nature of online text. It is common to see homophones being used in the representation of Written Cantonese. Some of these homophones might be more frequent than the perceived correct usage. These "incorrect characters" will generally be excluded from the dataset, although a separate list has been compiled for the purpose of identification of incorrect characters. If the editors judge that the incorrect forms are frequently used and must be included, a separate entry (with the "typo" label) will be created to redirect the users to the main entry with the conventional orthographic form.

### 4.3. Character Variants

Due to the ideographic nature of Han characters, various localities using Han characters have developed specific preferences in representing essentially the same character. To facilitate such preferences, different Unicode code points were created to represent some of these variants. For example, "溫" (0x6EAB) and "温" (0x6E29) are represented by different code points in Unicode, but in the context of Cantonese users, they both represent the same character.
Without an authority to define the use of traditional Han characters, Cantonese users tend to use variants interchangeably. For example, "温" is taught in schools in Hong Kong as the canonical variant (Lee, 2000); however, "溫" is often used on the Internet due to its existence in older encoding methods such as Big5, which did not include "温". Even government websites in Hong Kong (such as the Hong Kong Observatory) tend to use the Big-5-compatible "溫" character instead of the "correct" character "温".[3]
Given that Cantonese users treat such character variants interchangeably, a Cantonese dictionary must be able to recognize common variants of characters. For straightforward cases, we opted to pick one variant and normalize the characters into that variant. We started by using a mapping from

[3]However, a simple online search reveals that this preference is far from being consistent. Occasionally "温" is used on some government websites.

| Type | Etymology | Morpheme | Headword |
|---|---|---|---|
| Cantonese/ SWC-shared | 刀 | *dou1* "knife" | 刀 |
| English | CID | *si1aai1di1* "CID" | CID |
| English | download | *daang1lou1* "download" | Download / 單撈 |
| English | sorry | *so1* "sorry" | sor / 梳 |
| Mixed | P + 牌 | *pi1paai4* "probationary driving license" | P 牌 |
| Mixed | calculator + 機 | *keu1gei1* "calculator" | cal 機 |
| Mixed | 有 + point | *jau5pon1* "sensible, making good judgements" | 有 point |
| Onomatopoeia | (unknown) | *bi1li1baa1laa1* | 嗶哩叭啦 / bi li ba la |
| Onomatopoeia | (unknown) | *tiu4tiu2fing6* | 條條 fing / 條條揈 |
| Disputed | 奇離 | *ke4le4* "weird" | 騎呢 / 奇離 |
| Disputed | (unknown) | *liu1lang1* "uncommon; complicated" | 撩 lung / 叮嚨 |

Table 2: Examples of orthographic representations

OpenCC[4]. We removed most mappings with characters that are structurally different (as opposed to minor variants). We then applied the mapping onto our dictionary database, and checked for characters that are not on the List of Graphemes of Commonly-used Chinese Characters (Lee, 2000). Then, for each of these characters, we either manually added it to the list of accepted characters, or we added an entry to the variants mapping, or we made a conscious decision to leave it as-is as a special case of a rare or unusual character.

In the end, we produced a list of canonical characters, and a mapping of variants to canonical characters. We include these two items in our repository.

Note that, despite variants being usually interchangeable, there are exceptions. Names are one common case. For example, the name of the HSBC bank "滙豐 *wui6fung1*"[5] is not supposed to be written as "匯豐", in spite of the second form being the conventional character for this morpheme. For a dictionary, the use of proper names in the definition and explanation texts is rare, so we have not handled them explicitly. We would imagine that to process variants in corpora that include proper names, an additional step of identifying proper names would be required to keep them intact.

To avoid over-aggressive normalization, we err on the side of caution. We actually maintain two variant maps, the first we call a "safe" map, so called because we believe the variants can be safely used interchangeably. This safe map mostly contains glyph-level "interchangeable variants" (異寫字), which involve variation in minor stroke display (e.g. 說 vs 説) or configuration (e.g. 啟 vs 啓) rather than differences in structural components (e.g. 惗 vs 諗, 綫 vs 線). We use this "safe" map to automatically normalize variant characters in our database (and in this public dataset).

Other known non-canonical variant characters have been added to a much longer "unsafe" map. These characters should be avoided unless the use is justified, e.g. in proper names or certain combinations. A warning message will be displayed when an editor tries to use one of these characters in an entry, so that they can replace them with the canonical variant.

## 5. Pronunciation

The dictionary uses the Linguistic Society of Hong Kong Cantonese romanisation scheme (also known as "Jyutping" or "LSHK Jyutping"). This is the most common Cantonese romanisation scheme in education and research contexts, which is also employed in *HKCanCor*, *Cifu*, *Cantomap* and the *Unihan* database. Our system allows all combinations of initials and rhymes listed in LSHK 1993 and its 2018 expanded rhyme set, as well as nucleus-coda combinations that are attested but not officially recognized, e.g. -oem.

Pronunciations for the vast majority of the entries follow the LSHK schema. The small number of loanwords that cannot be represented in traditional Cantonese phonology will be recorded using an augmented version of the original LSHK sys-

[4]The OpenCC Hong Kong variant map is available at `https://github.com/BYVoid/OpenCC/blob/master/data/dictionary/HKVariants.txt`

[5]The Hongkong and Shanghai Banking Corporation, a bank with a major presence in Hong Kong.

tem, and these violating transliterations (e.g. the use of –s in the coda position) will be indicated by manually adding a "!" in front of the pronunciation.

To cater for phonological variation in the population of Hong Kong, certain compromises have been made. The pronunciation listed will be more conservative than actual usage. The mergers of the coda pairs {-n, -ng} and {-t, -k}, the onset pairs {ng-, ø-}, {n-, l-}, the tonal pairs {3, 6}, {2, 5}, {3, 5} have been reported (Fung and Lee, 2019; JyutJyuSi (JJS) Work Group, The Linguistic Society of Hong Kong, 2019), and the onset mergers are almost complete. However, the traditional forms will be listed in the dictionary, since the pre-merger pronunciation is considered the proper pronunciation and is expected in text-to-speech systems. However, the difference between the high-falling and high-level tones and other earlier phonological changes will not be represented in our data.

If there are multiple pronunciations for the same lexical item and are unrelated to recent phonological changes, all of them will be recorded in the entry.

## 6. Part-of-speech Tagging

The dictionary data is part-of-speech tagged, following the POS system in Tang (2015), and can be roughly mapped to the Universal Dependencies (UD) Cantonese-HK tag-set (Wong et al., 2017). By default, each entry should contain only one part-of-speech, with the exception of the following, which can be listed with multiple parts-of-speech in the same entry[6]:

1. verbal nouns, e.g. 默書 (*mak6syu1*, "dictation"), 尊稱 (*zyun1cing1*, "honorable title"), where the nominal usage is similar to that of a gerund;

2. some "好 (*hou2*)-nominal" constructions in the attribute-head form as adjectives when referring to qualities and as nouns when referring to nominals, e.g. 好人 (*hou2jan4*, "good person; kind, generous"), 好嘢 (*hou2je5*, "good stuff; excellent") and 好朋友 (*hou2pang4jau5*, "good friend; in deep, close friendship");

3. words that can be analyzed as either POS category and the choice is purely theory-driven.

Additional usage-related labels have also been provided in Table 4.

[6]Cases such as the extended usage of onomatopoeia are not considered as exceptions as they may not always share the exact meaning.

| POS | English Translation | UD |
|---|---|---|
| 名詞 | nouns | NOUN |
| 區別詞 | distinguishing words | ADJ |
| 數詞 | numerals | NUM |
| 量詞 | quantifiers | NOUN |
| 代詞 | pronouns | PRON, DET |
| 動詞 | verbs | VERB |
| 形容詞 | adjectives | ADJ |
| 副詞 | adverbs | ADV |
| 介詞 | prepositions | ADP |
| 連詞 | conjunctions | CCONJ, SCONJ |
| 助詞 | particles | PART |
| 擬聲詞 | onomatopoeia | INTJ |
| 感嘆詞 | interjection | INTJ |
| 詞綴 | affixes | PART, AUX |
| 語素 | morpheme | N/A |
| 語句 | expressions | N/A |

Table 3: Part-of-speech tags and their corresponding POS tags in UD-Cantonese

## 7. Definition Crafting

Word entries from the initial data contain only basic information (a written form, Jyutping pronunciation and sometimes reference text from other online resources). The definition needs to be crafted manually by our editors. Instead of preparing templates for all possible entries, our decision was to choose efficiency over consistency. These are some guiding instructions that we give to new editors.

- Is this a common, mid-range or rare word, in terms of perceived frequency in speech?
  - For a *common* word, list out different senses of the word with ample collocations and examples.
  - For a *mid-range* word, explain the word in plain language, and give one or two example sentences.
  - For a *rare* word, explain the word in a way that can describe its precise sense without using any other rare words.
- If it is an abstract concept, how would you explain it to a five year-old child?
- Is your definition too broad or restrictive for the word?

| Label | English |
|---|---|
| 粗俗 | vulgar |
| 俚語 | colloquial / slang |
| 爭議 | controversial |
| 潮語 | meme |
| 專名 | common name / proper noun |
| 術語 | jargon |
| 舊式 | obsolete |
| 香港 | hongkong |
| 大陸 | mainland |
| 台灣 | taiwan |
| 澳門 | macau |
| 日本 | japan |
| 外來語 | loanword |
| 書面語 | written |
| 口語 | verbal / spoken |
| 錯字 | wrong |
| 文言 | classical |
| 黃賭毒 | nsfw |
| 民間傳說 | folk etymology |

Table 4: Usage-related labels

Editors will need to decide what plain language and rare words refer to, and there is no need for a predefined controlled vocabulary, since there is not yet sufficient resources to compile one.

Certain categories, e.g. chemical elements, constellations, place names, names of languages and ethnic groups, are crafted based on a template. Entries created before the implementation of a template can be corrected afterwards. It is up to the editors to decide how the entries can be improved, through systematic checking or refining of a chosen categories initiated by individual editors.

## 8. Data Format

The dataset and other supporting files can be downloaded from this link: ***https://github.com/wordshk/data2021***

The CSV with the latest dictionary data comprises of the written form of entries, their pronunciations, explanations and examples. The CSV comes in five columns; the content of each column and a sample entry are shown in Table 5 and Table 6 respectively[7].

[7]The Entry-data (Column 3) can be parsed by an open source tool (`https://crates.io/crates/wordshk_tools`)

| | |
|---|---|
| ***Col1*** | Index |
| ***Col2*** | Orthographic representation & Jyutping |
| ***Col3*** | Entry-data (POS, Label, Synonyms, Antonyms, Explanation, and Examples) |
| ***Col4*** | Character variations |
| ***Col5*** | Review status |

Table 5: CSV Columns

| | |
|---|---|
| ***Col1*** | 76359 |
| ***Col2*** | 一般來說:jat1 bun1 loi4 syut3 |
| ***Col3*** | (pos: 語句)(label: 書面語)(sim: 一般而言)<br><explanation><br>yue: 用嚟引起下文，表示只係睇普遍情況，唔考慮個別例子<br>eng:in general, in most situations<br><eg><br>zho: 一般來說，男生都喜歡漂亮的女孩子。(jat1 bun1 loi4 syut3, naam4 sang1 dou1 hei2 fun1 piu3 loeng6 dik1 neoi5 haai4 zi2.)<br>yue: 一般嚟講，男仔都鍾意靚嘅女仔。(jat1 bun1 lai4 gong2, naam4 zai2 dou1 zung1 ji3 leng3 ge3 neoi5 zai2.)<br>eng:In general, boys like beautiful girls. |
| ***Col4*** | 一般來說 |
| ***Col5*** | OK |

Table 6: A Sample Entry

## 9. Licensing

In the exploratory phase of this project, we discovered that many institutions and people had attempted to create Cantonese dictionaries before us. Unlike languages that have established lexicography traditions and institutions supporting them, Cantonese dictionary projects have a tendency to become abandoned by their original owners. We suspect one reason is that, before the popularization of modern database technologies, and before the Internet made reference materials easily accessible, compilation of dictionaries from scratch required multiple years of dedication and highly focused attention, which is often beyond the capability of a single person or team.

We therefore made the assumption that even if the project is successful beyond our expectations, it will still benefit from arrangements to ensure the dictionary can continue to be developed even after

the original team has moved on.
Our license[8] is designed to do exactly that. Specifically:

1. Most non-commercial uses are allowed and do not require additional licensing.
2. Most copyright restrictions (including commercial use) expire in 10 years after publication[9]
3. Permission is given by default if the copyright owner does not respond to licensing requests.
4. Fair use and personal use exemptions are unambiguously defined.

We retained the right to license commercial use of the dictionary for two reasons: Firstly, we were funded exclusively by small donations from private individuals. While profit has never been a goal, reserving commercial rights may help sustain the project financially. Secondly, these restrictions discourage "forks" of the dictionary, preventing our work from being adapted to promote ideas that run counter to our tenets, in particular, folk etymology and fringe linguistic theories, which are unfortunately a common phenomenon with regard to Cantonese where there is no official body ready to make authoritative statements on the subject matter.
Note that the particular copy/version of our submitted data to this conference is also licensed under the Creative Commons Non Commercial license (CC-BY-NC 4.0). Although we believe our tailor-made license is superior for our purposes and goals (and we encourage data owners to consider adopting similar ideas into their licensing schemes), we nonetheless include a more commonly understood alternative for this particular version to avoid confusion and to facilitate sharing and collaboration.

## 10. Conclusion

This paper presents the design and compilation process of the first comprehensive dictionary for Cantonese that provides both Cantonese and English definitions. The project started as a lexicographical endeavor, which was later expanded into a language resource that serves both language teaching and natural language processing purposes.
Immediate use cases include simplistic (longest string matching) word segmentation and training of text-to-speech models with verified pronunciation mapping data. This project can fill the gap of the lack of written materials for the language due to its diglossic tradition by providing manually crafted example sentences for both common and rarer words, as well as Jyutping transcription for sentences. The size of the dictionary and its accompanying language materials have already surpassed existing openly available spoken corpora, and the project team continues to work on expanding the content of the project. Since all definitions are written in Cantonese (as opposed to other resources which normally provide definitions only in SWC or English), the dataset can be used in the construction or expansion of any semantic web projects or knowledge base. Similar techniques can also be applied to minority languages in the vicinity that use Han characters and may be facing similar issues. Future plans for the project include developing labels to store grammatical (morphological composition and syntactic properties) information and the conversion of the current format to follow the TEI Lex-0 standard.


## 11. Acknowledgments

The team would like to thank all contributors to the project, and all anonymous reviewers for their invaluable comments and suggestions.


## 12. Bibliographical References


Bacon-Shone, J., Bolton, K. R., and Luke, K. K. (2015). *Language use, proficiency and attitudes in Hong Kong.* Social Sciences Research Centre, the University of Hong Kong, Hong Kong.

Bergenholtz, H. and Tarp, S. (2003). Two opposing theories. On H.E. Wiegand's recent discovery of lexicographic functions. *HERMES - Journal of Language and Communication in Business*, 16(31):171–196.

Estellés-Arolas, E. and González-Ladrón-de Guevara, F. (2012). Towards an integrated crowdsourcing definition. *Journal of Information Science*, 38(2):189–200.

Fung, R. and Lee, C. (2019). Tone mergers in Hong Kong Cantonese: An asymmetry of production and perception. *The Journal of the Acoustical Society of America*, 146(5):EL424–EL430.

JyutJyuSi (JJS) Work Group, The Linguistic Society of Hong Kong. (2019). The recognition and acceptance of phonological variations in Cantonese and its justification. In *The 25th International Conference on Yue Dialects, Guangdong-Hong Kong-Macao University Alliance for Chinese.*

Lai, M. L. (2013). The linguistics landscape of Hong Kong after the change of sovereignty. *International Journal of Multilingualism*, 10(3):251–272.

Lau, C.-m. (2019). Building Cantonese dictionaries using crowdsourcing strategies: The words.hk project. In Tso A., editor, *Digital Humanities*


[8] `https://words.hk/base/hoifong/`

[9] as opposed to lifetime plus 50 years by default

*and New Ways of Teaching*, Digital Culture and Humanities, vol. 1. Springer, Singapore.

Lee, H.-m. (2000). *List of graphemes of commonly-used Chinese characters (revised version in 2000)*. The Hong Kong Institute of Education, Hong Kong.

Snow, D. B. (2004). *Cantonese as written language: The growth of a written Chinese vernacular*. Hong Kong University Press, Hong Kong.

Sproat, R., Gale, W., Shih, C., and Chang, N. (1996). A stochastic finite-state word-segmentation algorithm for Chinese. *Computational Linguistics*, 22(3).

Tang, S. W. (2015). *Lectures on Cantonese grammar*. Commercial Press, Hong Kong.

## 13. Language Resource References

Bauer, R. S. (2020). *ABC Cantonese-English Comprehensive Dictionary*. University of Hawaii Press.

CantoDict. (n.d.). *CantoDict*. `http://www.cantonese.sheik.co.uk/dictionary`.

Cantonese Computational Linguistics Infrastructure Development Group (CanCLID). (n.d.). *Rime-Cantonese Input Method*. `https://github.com/rime/rime-cantonese`.

CCCanto. (n.d.). *CCCanto*. `https://cantonese.org`.

Hutton, C. and Bolton, K. (2005). *A dictionary of Cantonese slang: The language of Hong Kong movies, street gangs and city life*. University of Hawaii Press.

Lai, R. and Winterstein, G. (2020). *Cifu: A frequency lexicon of Hong Kong Cantonese*. In Proceedings of the 12th Conference on Language Resources and Evaluation (LREC 2020), pp. 3069-3077, 1.0, ISLRN 321-291-722-262-7.

Leung, M. and Law, S. (2001). *HKCAC: The Hong Kong Cantonese Adult Language Corpus*. International Journal of Corpus Linguistics, 6(2): 305-325.

Luke, K. K. and Wong, M. L. (2015). *The Hong Kong Cantonese corpus: design and use*. Journal of Chinese Linguistics, 25(2015), 309-330.

Shen, F., Yu, W., Min, C., Ye, Q., Xia, C., Wang, T., and Wu, Y. (2021). *CyberCan: A new dictionary for Cantonese social media text segmentation*. https://doi.org/10.31235/osf.io/tyjr7.

Sio, J. U.-S. and da Costa, L. M. (2019). *Building the Cantonese Wordnet*. In Proceeding of the 10th Global Wordnet Conference, pp. 206-215, Wroclaw, Poland, July, Global Wordnet Association.

Winterstein, G., Tang, C., and Lai, R. (2020). *CantoMap: a Hong Kong Cantonese MapTask Corpus*. In Proceeding of the 12th Language Resources and Evaluation Conference, pp. 2899-2906, Marseille, European Language Resources Association, ISLRN 167-857-138-471-9.

Wong, T.-s., Gerdes, K., Leung, H., and Lee, J. (2017). *Quantitative comparative syntax on the Cantonese-Mandarin parallel dependency treebank*. In Proceeding of the Fourth International Conference on Dependency Linguistics (Depling 2017), pp. 266-275, Pisa, Italy, September, Linköping University Electronic Press.

# A. Appendix

## A.1. Data Card

**Dataset Name:** words.hk Cantonese Dictionary
**Dataset Developer:** words.hk
**Dataset License:** CC-BY-NC 4.0
**Link to Dataset:** `https://github.com/wordshk/data2021`
**Project website:** `https://words.hk`

## A.2. Ethical Considerations and Broader Impact

*Words.hk* is a dictionary created by the users, for the users of the Cantonese language. We aim to document the usage of Cantonese under a descriptive principle, and reject creation of a rigid dichotomy between "researchers" and "subjects"; all editors are equally empowered to present their experience with the language in this community-based model.

The vast majority of work was completed in a voluntary basis; editors are required to express consent before submitting their work. The consent form is integrated into the editing interface for visibility and written in simple Cantonese; as all of our editors are literate and familiar with the Internet, the consent form is considered sufficient for obtaining informed consent. Also included are clauses requiring the editor to transfer any and all applicable copyright to *words.hk*, in exchange for *words.hk* to release said work under our open data principles (see section 9) to avert copyright-related ambiguities and disputes.

Personal information collected from volunteers is limited to name and e-mail address for registration; editors are welcome to register and participate under a pseudonym. While the edits made by each editor are traceable to their account through the version history and activity log systems, such information will not be released to the public and is not included in the dataset. Contrarily, editors seeking due recognition for their contribution to the project may choose to be publicly acknowledged on the "About Us" page[10]. The displayed name can be customized by the editor entirely separate from the account username to prevent breach of privacy.

[10] `https://words.hk/base/about/`

As the use of real names is not considered necessary for illustrating the typical usage of the words, all sentences included in the dataset as examples are anonymized through replacing names with fictitious ones where applicable. Sentences selected or formed for examples are also carefully considered to avoid propagation of biases, harmful stereotypes and bigotry in general; words that are unavoidably offensive and derogatory in their usage, including slurs or pejoratives, will be specifically labelled as such (see Table 4).

In terms of broader impact, we hope this project can encourage more people to write in their own native language. Prior to the advent of *words.hk*, the use of written Cantonese was for the most part limited to corners of the Internet, and only for informal chatting; existing dictionaries contain only explanations in English or Standard Written Chinese. *words.hk* is the first Cantonese dictionary with explanations provided in both Cantonese and English, which proved the viability of using Cantonese in educational settings and paved the way for widespread use of written Cantonese. As of today, Cantonese is commonly used in a variety of ways, ranging from literature to government publications.

This project could also set an example on how non-expert community members can contribute to a monolingual dictionary. As discussed in section 2.2, editors need not to be proficient in every aspect and capable of crafting an entire entry by themselves before they can contribute to the project. Additionally, we also maintain several communication channels where associative members of the community, who are not directly involved with the editing process for one reason or another, could offer their views and comments. Editors would often raise questions and ask for opinions when they encounter uncertainties in the editing process. In this way, we can involve a greater share of the community beyond those who have the technical skills to work with the online system.

*Proceedings of the 1st Workshop on Dataset Creation for Lower-Resourced Languages (DCLRL) @LREC2022*, pages 63–67
Marseille, 24 June 2022


# LiSTra Automatic Speech Translation: English to Lingala Case Study

**Salomon Kabongo, Vukosi Marivate, Herman Kamper**
African Masters of Machine Intelligence, University of Pretoria, Stellenbosch University
skabenamualu@aimsammi.org, vukosi.marivate@cs.up.ac.za, kamperh@sun.ac.za

**Abstract**

In recent years there has been great interest in addressing the data scarcity of African languages and providing baseline models for different Natural Language Processing tasks (Orife et al., 2020). Several initiatives (Nekoto et al., 2020) on the continent uses the Bible as a data source to provide proof of concept for some NLP tasks. In this work, we present the Lingala Speech Translation (LiSTra) dataset, release a full pipeline for the construction of such dataset in other languages, and report baselines using both the traditional cascade approach (Automatic Speech Recognition - Machine Translation), and a revolutionary transformer based End-2-End architecture (Liu et al., 2020) with a custom interactive attention that allows information sharing between the recognition decoder and the translation decoder.

**Keywords:** NLP, Speech-to-text, Speech, Translation

## 1. Introduction

Automatic Speech Translation (AST) is the task of converting an utterance from a source language to transcription in a target language, such a task has several applications in real life. Success in this task will revolutionize online education, the majority of educational content available on e-learning platforms like Udacity, Edx, and Coursera among others are English-centric and this is a bottleneck to people with limited or no knowledge of English to have access to those contents. As a starting point in this direction, inspired by (Orife et al., 2020) we performed a proof of concept for Automatic Speech Translation from a higher resources language (English) to a lower one, Lingala in this case.

Lingala (Ngala) (Lingala: lingála) is a Bantu language spoken throughout the northwestern part of the Democratic Republic of the Congo (Wikipedia contributors, 2020) and a large part of the Republic of the Congo. It is spoken to a lesser degree in Angola, the Central African Republic, and Southwest & Southcentral Republic of South Sudan. There are over 40 million lingalaphones [1].

Based on a study made in 2009 by youthpolicy[2] the population of the Democratic Republic of the Congo (DRC) is young and rejuvenating over 68% of people aged less than 25 years, a majority of whom live in rural areas (over 60 %), this situation has not much changed since. This young population is not always able to speak the official language (French) and this work is a start to making educational materials available to them.

One bottleneck in experimenting on ASR especially for low resources languages has been lack of aligned data, inspired by the Masakhane (Orife et al., 2020) initiative and (Agic and Vulic, 2020) we introduce in this paper **LiSTra**[3] which stands for **Lingala Speech Translation** a dataset of reading of the Bible, the corresponding transcription in English as well as the Lingala translation. The choice of the bible as a data source is motivated by missionary work on the African continent, which made available the transcription and the translation alignments. Despite the religious nature of the content in the Bible, some of its recent version provide a good starting point for experimentation in several NLP tasks.

The traditional approach in AST is what is known as a pipeline system where we first do Automatic Speech Recognition(ASR), then feed the output into a Machine Translation (MT) system, one pitfall in this approach is the error propagation (not back-propagation) that arise due to the fact that the 2 components are trained independently. In this work we will release a baseline for AST both in a pipeline (ASR -> MT) as well as in an end-to-end setting, in addition, we published what happens to be at the best of our knowledge the first dataset for neural speech translation from English to Lingala. Our main contributions are summarized as follows:

- Release a detailed methodology to create new datasets for Automatic Speech Translation (AST) for low resource languages which can be also useful both for Machine Translation (MT) and Automatic Speech Recognition tasks independently.
- Provide a baseline for AST for English-to-Lingala in both pipeline and end-2-end settings

## 2. Related work

The recent breakthroughs in end-to-end architectures in Machine Translation and Speech Recognition have lead to the investigation of having end-to-end architectures for Automatic Speech Translation (Bérard et al., 2016). Historically Automatic Speech Translation (ASR) was done in two steps: we first do automatic speech recognition on the source language and next feed the obtained transcription into a separate machine translation model, this is sometimes referred to in the literature as Cascade Speech Translation (Cascade-ST). One immediate

[1]https://en.wikipedia.org/wiki/Lingala

[2]https://www.youthpolicy.org/factsheets/country/congo-kinshasa.

[3]`https://github.com/Kabongosalomon/LiSTra`

issue with this approach is the error-propagation (not back-propagation).
Since the first AST proof of concept proposed by (Zong et al., 1999) there has been interesting works to improve on the state of the art, this is mostly because of it business side as well as community impact, for example, people with disability can use the outcome of this task to learn and get access to information. Due to the difficulty of the accessibility of aligned data, there has been some attempt to perform AST without source transcription (Bérard et al., 2016).
African languages have been for a long time left behind in the Major NLP conference. Recently, there have been initiatives like Deep Learning Indaba[4] and Data Science Africa[5] among others that aim to focus on solving and addressing African's problems using Machine Learning learning and AI. These movements have given birth to Masakhane which is an African initiative that focuses on Natural Language Processing related problem in the continent (Orife et al., 2020). The Masakhane initiative has been mostly at it current state making use of the JW300 dataset (Agic and Vulic, 2020) which is basically made of religious text that is inherently aligned on chapter and verse level and this has allowed the community to publish (Nekoto et al., 2020) baselines for several languages which were before untouched despite the number of people speaking and using them.
Our work in this paper aligned mostly with this work (Liu et al., 2020), that implemented a revolutionary architecture based on transformers that allow having 2 decoders that communicate among themselves in an intuitive way to perform Automatic Speech Translation but in our context, we will experiment with this same architecture in a low-resource setting to rapport its performance for English to Lingala translation.

## 3. Dataset

In the $20^{th}$ century, data is considered to be the new oil (Arthur, 2021), especially in supervised learning regimes where we can't talk of Machine learning without it. Africa currently has 2144 living languages (Eberhard et al., 2019). Despite this, African languages account for a small fraction of available language resources, and NLP research rarely considers African languages (Nekoto et al., 2020). Inspired by the work by (Orife et al., 2020) and (Agic and Vulic, 2020) we made use of the structural form of the bible, to create LiSTra. Let $D = \{\mathrm{S}^{(j)}, \mathrm{E}^{(j)}, \mathrm{L}^{(j)}\}_{j=1}^{|D|}$ the dataset that we would like to create, with $S$ the speech utterance (in English), $E$ the corresponding transcription (in Lingala) and $L$ the gold truth Lingala translation.

### 3.1. Sources and structure

LiSTra is a systemic crawl of the new testament both at the jw.org for Lingala translation and bible.is for speech and English transcription. The bible is originally aligned by chapter and several websites provide read speech of the all bible in several languages. One big challenge with doing ASR research with the bible data in its original format is the alignment at the chapter, which usually is long and not suitable for ASR.
Automatic Speech Recognition (ASR) also known as Speech-Text-To (STT) has been historically a close domain compare to others due to the expenses to train a fully working system and the difficulty that came with it, this leads to having only big tech companies working in this field.
In the next section, we will present our procedure to transform the data in the adequate format for Automatic Speech Translation (AST), from the web crawling step to the ready-to-use AST format.

### 3.2. Curation

The first step consists of scrapping the text and downloading audios files corresponding to the languages pair at study, English-Lingala in our case. We used the *English Standard Version - FCBH Audio Audio Non-Drama New Testament* from bible.is[6] and the *Biblia Libongoli ya Mokili ya Sika*[7] version for the Lingala version from the jw.org which will be used for the aligned translation[8].
The bible text being systematically organized by verses, make it perfect to keep the same alignment for automatic speech translation but the bottleneck remains the fact that all audios reading of the bible are only at book level with no way to manually split it at the verse level.
To split the chapter level reading waves at verse level we made use of the automatic segmentation service WebMAUSBasic of the Bavarian Archive for Speech Signals (BAS)[9] project similarly to (Boito et al., 2019). The code to perform this segmentation using a jupyter notebook can be found here Anonymous.
Given that the text is crawled from two different websites (jw.org and bible.is) and in two different versions, we noticed inconsistancy on some books that don't have the same number of verses and we decided to drop the concerned cases.

## 4. Experiments and Results

We have created what is at the best of our knowledge the first baseline for Automatic Speech Translation (AST) from English to Lingala, in both Cascade and End-2-End configuration[10].

[4]https://deeplearningindaba.com
[5]http://www.datascienceafrica.org/
[6]https://www.faithcomesbyhearing.com/audio-bible-resources/mp3-downloads
[7]https://www.jw.org/ln/Biblioteke/biblia/bi12/mikanda/matai/2/
[8]constrained by the licensing we have not released the audios files
[9]https://www.bas.uni-muenchen.de/Bas/BasHomeeng.html
[10]Anonymous

| | LiSTra | | | |
|---|---|---|---|---|
| Text language Source | Split | Examples | Avg. text length | Total Unique Words |
| English (En) | train | 23717 | 24.2712 | 13139 |
| | test | 5930 | 24.2076 | 7772 |
| Text language Target | Split | Examples | Avg. text length | Total Unique Words |
| Lingala (ln) | train | 23717 | 25.9165 | 16808 |
| | test | 5930 | 25.7489 | 8940 |
| Speech Source | Split | Examples | Avg. audio length (seconds) | Total numb. hours |
| English (.wav) | train | 23717 | 9.2880 | 61 |
| | test | 5930 | 9.2715 | 15 |

Table 1: Data statistics of LiSTra

### 4.1. Automatic Speech Translation: Cascade

The Cascade architecture is made of two separate models as described in Figure 1, a pre-trained Sirelo[11] Model and a traditional transformer-based Machine translation architecture which receive the output of the former one to perform Automatic Speech Translation.

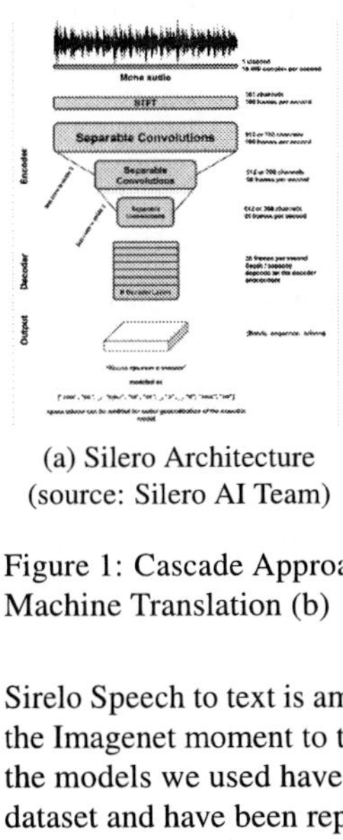

(a) Silero Architecture (source: Silero AI Team)

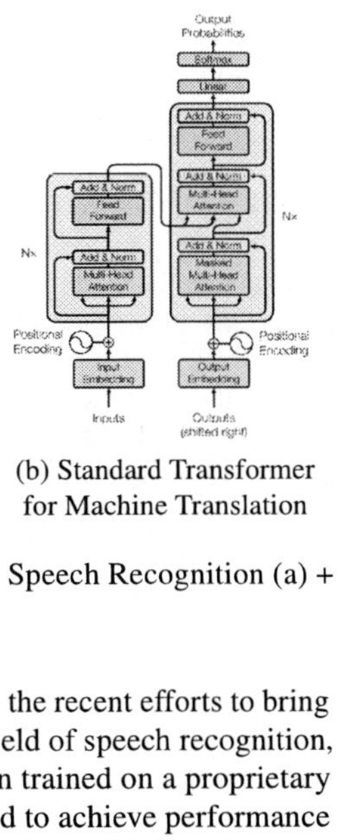


(b) Standard Transformer for Machine Translation

Figure 1: Cascade Approach : Speech Recognition (a) + Machine Translation (b)

Sirelo Speech to text is among the recent efforts to bring the Imagenet moment to the field of speech recognition, the models we used have been trained on a proprietary dataset and have been reported to achieve performance that sometimes surpasses the state-of-the-art in some languages (Veysov, 2020).
The MT model [12] is based on the standard transformer architecture, but with a dimensionality of input and output of 256, refer on the original paper (Vaswani et al., 2017) as $d_{model}$ and a inner-layer dimension $d_{ff}$ of 512.
We pre-trained the Machine Translation model on the JW300 dataset (Agic and Vulic, 2020) and train further on LiSTra data. The recognized waves from silero are then fed into the trained MT to obtain our Speech translation output.

### 4.2. Automatic Speech Translation: end-2-end

In the end-2end setting, we used a transformer-based model3, that is made of one encoder and two decoders as shown in figure 2. This architecture has shown promising results recently (Liu et al., 2020) specially due to the interaction between the recognition decoder and the translation decoder.

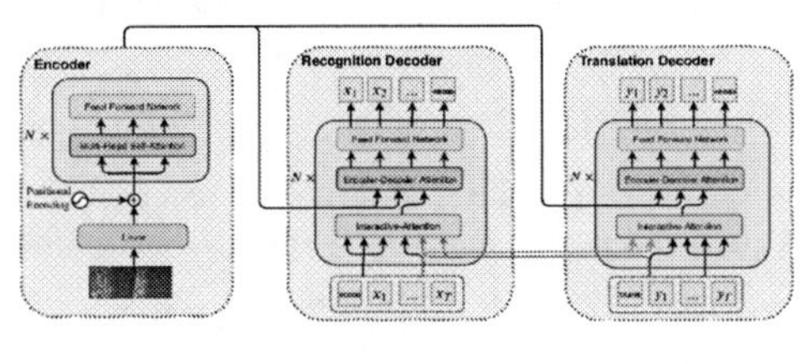


Figure 2: Synchronous AST Architecture (Liu et al., 2020)

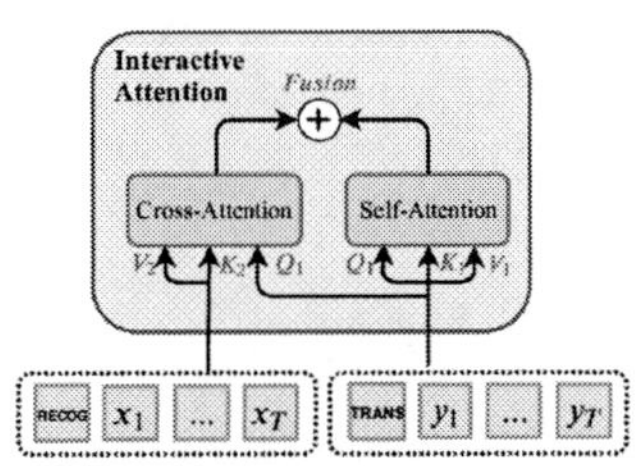


Figure 3: Interactive Attention

[11]https://github.com/snakers4/silero-models
[12]https://github.com/bentrevett/pytorch-seq2seq

| | wait-1 | | | wait-2 | | | wait-3 | | |
|---|---|---|---|---|---|---|---|---|---|
| Architecture | WER ↓ | BLEU (en) ↑ | BLEU (ln) ↑ | WER ↓ | BLEU (en) ↑ | BLEU (ln) ↑ | WER ↓ | BLEU (en) ↑ | BLEU (ln) ↑ |
| Pipeline[13] | 8.27 | 84.90 | 13.92 | x | x | x | x | x | x |
| End-2-End | 8.06 | 84.40 | 26.45 | **7.81** | **84.90** | **28.52** | 7.87 | 84.73 | 26.99 |

Table 2: Results : Experimentation for different value of $k$

| | vocab_src_size | vocab_tgt_size | train_steps | decode_alpha | gpu_mem_fraction |
|---|---|---|---|---|---|
| Transformer_params | 30000 | 30000 | 80000 | 0.6 | 0.95 |

Table 3: LiSTra parameters, in addition to traditional transformer parameters

The interactive attention sub-layer is basically the main revolutionary idea of this architecture, the intuition is to allow systematic information sharing between the transcription and the translation decoders. The right side of the Interactive Attention block is not very different from the vanilla attention formalism, but the difference is with the second bloc that queries from the gold translation.
The intuition is to provide direct context from the translation/recognition input to the "Cross-Attention" that will supply additional information to the recognition/translation decoder. The Interactive Attention box fuses the self-attention to the Cross-Attention using weighted addition but more complex fuse functions can be explored in future work.
Formally, the interactive attention can be written mathematically as follow :

$$\texttt{Attention\_transcription}\,(\mathbf{Q}_1, \mathbf{K}_1, \mathbf{V}_1) = softmax\left(\frac{\mathbf{Q}_1 \mathbf{K}_1{}^T}{\sqrt{d_{k_1}}}\right)\mathbf{V}_1 \quad (1)$$

$$\texttt{Attention\_translation}\,(\mathbf{Q}_1, \mathbf{K}_2, \mathbf{V}_2) = softmax\left(\frac{\mathbf{Q}_1 \mathbf{K}_2{}^T}{\sqrt{d_{k_2}}}\right)\mathbf{V}_2 \quad (2)$$

Where

- $Q_1$, $K_1$ $V_1$ is the query, key, and value from the translation task, and $V_2$ $K_2$ is the value, key of the transcription task respectively.
- $d_{k_1}$ *and* $d_{k_2}$ is the dimension of the $K_1$ and $K_2$, respectively.

We can notice from the equation 1 that the hidden representation of the recognition task have as query the information for the translation ground truth, the final representation of the interactive attention will be written as :

$$Interactive\ attention = Attention\_translation + \lambda \times Attention\_transcription$$

With $\lambda$ a hyper-parameter that allows controlling the amount of information shared between the two tasks.
The prediction probability of both the translation and transcription can be formalized as

$$\log P(\mathrm{E} \mid \mathrm{S}, \mathrm{L}) = \sum_{i=0}^{N-1} \log p\left(e_i \mid e_{<i}, \mathrm{S}, l_{<i}\right) \quad (3)$$

$$\log P(\mathrm{L} \mid \mathrm{S}, \mathrm{E}) = \sum_{i=0}^{N-1} \log p\left(l_i \mid l_{<i}, \mathrm{S}, e_{<i}\right) \quad (4)$$

Where

- $S$ is the speech utterance
- $E$ is the corresponding aligned English Transcription
- $L$ is the corresponding aligned Lingala Transcription

Our objective function is then expressed as

$$L(\theta) = \sum_{j=1}^{|D|} \left(\log P\left(\mathrm{E}^{(j)} \mid \mathrm{S}^{(j)}, \mathrm{L}^{(j)}\right) + \log P\left(\mathrm{L}^{(j)} \mid \mathrm{S}^{(j)}, \mathrm{E}^{(j)}\right)\right) \quad (5)$$

Given that the Text to Speech task is often more difficult than Automatic Speech Recognition similarly to (Liu et al., 2020) we used the $wait - k$ policy approach that basically allows waiting for a certain time to allow the recognition decoder to transcribe some words before it can start translating. Table 3 summarizes our experiments with different values of $k$ and we empirically realized that we have better performance for $k = 2$.
The End-2-End architecture was pre-trained for 50000-steps on TED_Speech_Translation[14] which was constructed by collecting speech and corpus from TED talks and then fine-tuned on LiSTra, this is arguable the reason we have the recognition decoder with better performance than the translation one, pre-training the translation decoder is left for future work.
As observed in Table 3 for $k = 2$ we have a better Word Error Rate (WER) and BLEU score for both the recognition and translation decoder, in other words slowing down the translation decoder with a factor of 2 gives the translation decoder more context to provide better performance.

[14]http://www.nlpr.ia.ac.cn/cip/dataset.htm

Compared with the Machine Translation results from Masakhane (Orife et al., 2020) our translation decoder is performing poorly, probably because we don't have enough training examples and need to pre-trained the translation decoder separately to increase its performance. One probable direction to increase and produce unbiased data may be the use of platforms like Mozilla Common Voice or similar technology that can use a human-in-the-loop approach to collect qualitative data.

## 5. Conclusion

In this work, we presented LiSTra, the first dataset for automatic speech translation from English to Lingala, and a full pipeline to allow researchers working on low-resource languages to create a similar dataset for their language. Despite the dataset been biased toward religious languages this can serve as a starting dataset for proof of concept and can, later on, be improved with additional data.
In addition, we reported baselines in both Pipeline and End-2-End architecture and concluded that the End-2-End architecture performs quite well despite the limited amount of data.
For future work, one could extend LiSTra with other data sources, pre-train both the recognition and the translation decoder separately which may probably lead to better performances overall.

## 6. Bibliographical References


Agic, Ž. and Vulic, I. (2020). Jw300: A wide-coverage parallel corpus for low-resource languages.

Arthur, Charles; editor, t. .-.-. (2021). "tech giants may be huge, but nothing matches big data". *The Guardian. ISSN 0261-3077.*

Bérard, A., Pietquin, O., Servan, C., and Besacier, L. (2016). Listen and translate: A proof of concept for end-to-end speech-to-text translation. *arXiv preprint arXiv:1612.01744.*

Boito, M. Z., Havard, W. N., Garnerin, M., Ferrand, É. L., and Besacier, L. (2019). Mass: A large and clean multilingual corpus of sentence-aligned spoken utterances extracted from the bible. *arXiv preprint arXiv:1907.12895.*

Eberhard, D. M., Simons, G. F., and Fennig, C. D. (2019). *Ethnologue: Languages of Asia.* SIL International.

Liu, Y., Zhang, J., Xiong, H., Zhou, L., He, Z., Wu, H., Wang, H., and Zong, C. (2020). Synchronous speech recognition and speech-to-text translation with interactive decoding. In *AAAI*, pages 8417–8424.

Nekoto, W., Marivate, V., Matsila, T., Fasubaa, T., Fagbohungbe, T., Akinola, S. O., Muhammad, S., Kabongo Kabenamualu, S., Osei, S., Sackey, F., Niyongabo, R. A., Macharm, R., Ogayo, P., Ahia, O., Berhe, M. M., Adeyemi, M., Mokgesi-Selinga, M., Okegbemi, L., Martinus, L., Tajudeen, K., Degila, K., Ogueji, K., Siminyu, K., Kreutzer, J., Webster, J., Ali, J. T., Abbott, J., Orife, I., Ezeani, I., Dangana, I. A., Kamper, H., Elsahar, H., Duru, G., Kioko, G., Espoir, M., van Biljon, E., Whitenack, D., Onyefuluchi, C., Emezue, C. C., Dossou, B. F. P., Sibanda, B., Bassey, B., Olabiyi, A., Ramkilowan, A., Öktem, A., Akinfaderin, A., and Bashir, A. (2020). Participatory research for low-resourced machine translation: A case study in African languages. In *Findings of the Association for Computational Linguistics: EMNLP 2020*, pages 2144–2160, Online, November. Association for Computational Linguistics.

Orife, I., Kreutzer, J., Sibanda, B., Whitenack, D., Siminyu, K., Martinus, L., Ali, J. T., Abbott, J., Marivate, V., Kabongo, S., et al. (2020). Masakhane–machine translation for africa. *arXiv preprint arXiv:2003.11529.*

Vaswani, A., Shazeer, N., Parmar, N., Uszkoreit, J., Jones, L., Gomez, A. N., Kaiser, Ł., and Polosukhin, I. (2017). Attention is all you need. *Advances in neural information processing systems*, 30:5998–6008.

Veysov, A. (2020). Toward's an imagenet moment for speech-to-text. *The Gradient.*

Wikipedia contributors. (2020). Lingala — Wikipedia, the free encyclopedia. [Online; accessed 30-October-2020].

Zong, C., Huang, T., and Bo, X. (1999). Technical analysis on automatic spoken language translation systems. *Journal of Chinese Information Processing*, 13(2):55–65.

*Proceedings of the 1st Workshop on Dataset Creation for Lower-Resourced Languages (DCLRL) @LREC2022*, pages 68–75
Marseille, 24 June 2022


# Ara-Women-Hate: An annotated corpus dedicated to Hate speech detection against women in the Arabic community

**Imane Guellil[1], Ahsan Adeel[3], Faical Azouaou[2],Mohamed Boubred[4],Yousra Houichi[5], Akram Abdelhaq Moumna[2]**
[1]University of Edinburgh, Edinburgh, United Kingdom
[2]Laboratoire des Méthodes de Conception des Systèmes (LMCS), Ecole nationale Supérieure d'Informatique, BP 68M, 16309, Oued-Smar, Alger, Algérie,
[3]School of Mathematics and Computer Science, University of Wolverhampton,
[4]Capgemini, France
[5]Factory Digitale, Algeria,
imane.guellil@ed.ac.uk

**Abstract**

In this paper, an approach for hate speech detection against women in the Arabic community on social media (e.g. Youtube) is proposed. In the literature, similar works have been presented for other languages such as English. However, to the best of our knowledge, not much work has been conducted in the Arabic language. A new hate speech corpus (Arabic_fr_en) is developed using three different annotators. For corpus validation, three different machine learning algorithms are used, including deep Convolutional Neural Network (CNN), long short-term memory (LSTM) network and Bi-directional LSTM (Bi-LSTM) network. Simulation results demonstrate the best performance of CNN model which achieved an F1-score up to 86% for the unbalanced corpus as compared to LSTM and Bi-LSTM.

**Keywords:** Hate speech detection; Arabic language; Sexism detection; Deep learning

## 1. Introduction

With the online proliferation of hate speech, an important number of research studies have been presented in the last few years. The majority of these studies detect general hate speech (Burnap and Williams, 2014; Davidson et al., 2017; Wiegand et al., 2018) and focused on detecting sexism and racism on social media (Waseem and Hovy, 2016; Pitsilis et al., 2018; Kshirsagar et al., 2018). In contrast, only a few studies (Saha et al., 2018) focused on the detection of hate speech against women (only by distinguishing between hateful and non hateful comments). However, almost all studies are dedicated to English where other languages such as Arabic is also one of the four top used languages on the Internet (Guellil et al., 2018c; Guellil et al., 2018a; Guellil et al., 2021)). To bridge the gap, in this paper, we propose a novel approach to detect hate speech against women in Arabic community.

## 2. Background

### 2.1. Hate speech

Different definitions of hate speech are adopted by the research literature. However, the definition of (Nockleby, 2000) was recently largely used by many authors such as, (De Smedt et al., 2018; Schmidt and Wiegand, 2017; Zhang et al., 2018; Madisetty and Desarkar, 2018) and (Zhang and Luo, 2018). According to Nockleby, *"Hate speech is commonly defined as any communication that disparages or defames a person or a group on the basis of some characteristic such as race, color, ethnicity, gender, sexual orientation, nationality, religion, or other characteristics"* (Nockleby, 2000). For illustrating how this hate can be presented in textual exchange, (Schmidt and Wiegand, 2017) provided some examples:

- Go fucking kill yourself and die already useless ugly pile of shit scumbag.
- The Jew Faggot Behind The Financial Collapse.
- Hope one of those bitches falls over and breaks her leg.

Based on the recent survey of (Schmidt and Wiegand, 2017), we decided to use the term *Hate speech* (which is the most commonly used) rather than other terms present in the literature for the same phenomenon such as: *abusive speech* (Andrusyak et al., 2018; Gorrell et al., 2018), *offensive language* (Risch et al., 2018; Pitsilis et al., 2018; Puiu and Brabete, 2019) or *cyberbullying* (Dadvar and Eckert, 2018; Van Hee et al., 2018). According to Chetty and Alathur (Chetty and Alathur, 2018), hate speech is categorized into four categories: gendered hate speech (including any form of misogyny, sexism, etc), religious hate speech (including any kind of religious discrimination, such as: Islamic sects, anti-Christian, anti-Hinduism, etc), racist hate speech (including any sort of racial offence or tribalism, xenophobia, etc) and disability (including any sort of offence to an individual suffering from health which limits to do some of the life activities) (Al-Hassan and Al-Dossari, 2019). However, this survey neglected a category which could influence important international outcomes which is political hate speech. Political hate speech can be referred to any abuse, offence, injuries regarding politicians.

## 2.2. Arabic in social media

Arabic is one of the six official languages of the United Nations[1] (Eisele and Chen, 2010; Ziemski et al., 2016; Guellil and Azouaou, 2016). It is the official language of 22 countries. It is spoken by more than 400 million speakers. Arabic is also recognized as the 4th most used language of the Internet (Al-Kabi et al., 2016; Boudad et al., 2017). All the works in the literature (Habash, 2010; Farghaly and Shaalan, 2009; Harrat et al., 2017; Guellil et al., 2019; ?; Guellil et al., 2017a) classify Arabic in three main varieties: 1) Classical Arabic (CA) which is the form of Arabic language used in literary texts. The Quran [2] is considered to be the highest form of CA text (Sharaf and Atwell, 2012a). 2) Modern Standard Arabic (MSA) which is used for writing as well as formal conversations. 3) Dialectal Arabic which is used in daily life communication, informal exchanges, etc (Boudad et al., 2017). However, Arabic speakers on social media, discussion forums and Short Messaging Service (SMS) often use a non standard romanization called 'Arabizi' (Darwish, 2014; Bies et al., 2014). For example, the Arabic sentence: راني فرحانة, which means I am happy, is written in Arabizi as 'rani fer7ana'. Hence, Arabizi is an Arabic text written using Latin characters, numerals and some punctuation (Darwish, 2014; Guellil et al., 2018a). Moreover, most of Arabic people are bilingual, where the Mashreq side (Egypt, Gulf, etc) often use English and the Maghreb side (Tunisia, Algeria, etc) often use French, as second language. This linguistic richness contributes to increase a well known phenomenon on social media which is *code switching*. Therefore, Arabic pages also contain messages such as: "راني super فرحانة" or "راني very فرحانة" meaning I am very happy. In addition, messages purely written in French or in English are also possible.

Many studies have been proposed, in order to deal with Arabic and Arabizi (Darwish, 2014; Guellil et al., 2017b). Extracting opinions, analysing sentiments and emotion represent an emerging research area for Arabic and its dialects (Guellil et al., 2017c; Guellil et al., 2018b; Imane et al., 2019). However, few studies are dedicated to analyze extreme negative sentiments such as hate speech. Arabic hate speech detection is relatively a new research area where we were able to to collect only few works. these approaches are described in more details in the following section.

[1] http://www.un.org/en/sections/about-un/official-languages/

[2] The Quran is a scripture which, according to Muslims, is the verbatim words of Allah containing over 77,000 words revealed through Archangel Gabriel to Prophet Muhammad over 23 years beginning in 610 CE. It is divided into 114 chapters of varying sizes, where each chapter is divided into verses, adding up to a total of 6,243 verses. The work of Sharaf et al. (Sharaf and Atwell, 2012b)

# 3. Related work

## 3.1. Hate speech detection

### 3.1.1. General hate speech detection

Burnap and Williams (Burnap and Williams, 2014) investigated the spread of hate speech after Lee Rigby murder in UK. The authors collected 450,000 tweets and randomly picked 2,000 tweets for the manual annotation conducted by CrowdFlower (CF) workers[3]. Each tweet was annotated by 4 annotators. The final dataset contains 1,901 annotated tweets. The authors used three classification algorithmsand the best achieved classification results were up to 0.77 (for F1-score) using the Binary Logistic Regression (BLR). Davidson et al. (Davidson et al., 2017) distinguished between hateful and offensive speech by applying the Logistic Regression (LR) classifier The authors automatically extracted a set of tweets and manually annotated 24,802, randomly selected by CF workers. Their model achieved an F1 score of 0.90 but suffered poor generalization capability with up to 40% misclassification. Weigand et al. (Wiegand et al., 2018) also focused on the detection of abusive language. The authors used several features and lexical resources to build an abusive lexicon. Afterwards, constructed lexicon in an SVM classification was used. In this work, publicly available datasets were used (Razavi et al., 2010; Warner and Hirschberg, 2012; Waseem and Hovy, 2016).

It is to be noted that all the aforementioned studies have been conducted with English language. However, a few other studies in some other languages are also conducted recently such as Italian (Del Vigna12 et al., 2017), German (Köffer et al., 2018), Indonesian (Alfina et al., 2017), Russian (Andrusyak et al., 2018). However, only a limited number of researches have focused on hate speech detection in Arabic language. Abozinadah et al. (Abozinadah et al., 2015) evaluated different machine learning algorithms to detect abusive Arabic tweets. The authors manually selected and annotated 500 accounts associated to the abusive extracted tweets and used three classification algorithms The best results were obtained with the Naîve Bayes (NB) classifier with F1-score up to 0.90. Mubarek et al. (Mubarak et al., 2017) focused on the detection and classification of the obscene and offensive Arabic tweets. The authors used the Log Odds Ration (LOR) For evaluation, the authors manually annotated 100 tweets and obtained a F1-score up to 0.60. Haidar et al. (Haidar et al., 2017) proposed a system to detect and stop cyberbullying on social media. The authors manually annotated a dataset of 35,273 tweets from Middle East Region (especially from Lebanon, Syria, Gulf Area and Egypt). For classification, the authors used SVM and NB and obtained the best results with SVM achieving F1-score up to 0.93. More recently, Alakrot et al. (Alakrot et al., 2018) described a step by step

[3] https://www.figure-eight.com/

construction of an offensive dataset of Youtube Arabic comments. The authors extracted 167,549 Youtube comments from 150 Youtube video. For annotation, 16,000 comments were randomly picked (annotated by 3 annotators). Finally, Albadi et al. (Albadi et al., 2018) addressed the detection of Religious Arabic hate speech. The authors manually annotated 6,136 tweets (where 5,569 were used for training and 567 for testing). For feature extraction, AraVec (Soliman et al., 2017) was used.

#### 3.1.2. Sexism detection (Hate speech against women)

Waseem et al. (Waseem and Hovy, 2016) used LR classification algorithm to detect sexism and racism on social media. The authors manually annotated a dataset containing 16,914 tweets where 3,383 tweets are for sexist content, 1,972 for racist content, and 11,559 for neither sexist or racism. For dataset generation, the authors used Twitter API for extracting tweets containing some keywords related to women. The authors achieved F1-score up to 0.73. The work of Waseem et al. (Waseem and Hovy, 2016) is considered as a benchmark by many researchers (Al-Hassan and Al-Dossari, 2019; Pitsilis et al., 2018; Kshirsagar et al., 2018). The idea of Pitsilis et al. (Pitsilis et al., 2018) is to employ a neural network solution composed of multiple Long-Short-Term-Memory (LSTM) based classifiers in order to detect sexism and racism in social media. The authors carried out many experiments achieving the best F1-score of 0.93. Kshirsagar et al. (Kshirsagar et al., 2018) also focused on racism and sexism detection and their approach is also based on neural networks. However, in this work, the author also used word embedding for extracting feature combining with a Muli-Layer Perception (MLP) based classifier. The best achieved F1-score was up to 0.71. Saha et al. (Saha et al., 2018) presented a model to detect hate speech against women. The authors used several algorithms to extract features such as bag-of-words (BOW), TF-IDF and sentence embeddings with different classification algorithms such as LR, XGBoost and CatBoost. The best achieved F1-score was 0.70 using LR classifier. Zhang et al. (Zhang et al., 2018) proposed a hybrid model combining CNN and LSTM to detect hate speech. The authors applied their model to 7 datasets where 5 are publicly available (Waseem and Hovy, 2016; Waseem, 2016; Gambäck and Sikdar, 2017; Park and Fung, 2017; Davidson et al., 2017).

### 3.2. Motivation and contribution

The hate speech detection on social media is relatively new but an important topic. There are very few publicly available corpora mostly dedicated to English. Even for English, less than 10 resources are publicly available. More recently, researchers have presented work in other languages including German, Italian, Arabic. However, most of the work focuses on detecting a general hate speech not against a specific community. In Arabic, only 5 research studies are presented in the literature which are mainly focused on Twitter. This paper focuses on Youtube which is the second biggest social media platform, after Facebook, with 1.8 billion users (Kallas, 2017; Alakrot et al., 2018). The major contributions of this study are: Development of a novel hate speech corpus against women containing MSA and Algerian dialect, written in Arabic, Arabizi, French, and English. The corpus constitutes 5,000 manually annotated comments. For corpus validation, three deep learning algorithms (CNN, LSTM, and bi-LSTM) are used for hate speech classification. For feature extraction, algorithms such as word2vec, FasText, etc., are used.

## 4. Methodology

### 4.1. Dataset creation

#### 4.1.1. Data collection

Youtube comments related to videos about women are used. Feminine adjective such as: جميلة meaning beautiful, جَايحة meaning stupid or كلبة meaning a dog are targeted. A video on Youtube is recognised by a unique identifier (*video_id*). For example the video having an id equal to *"TJ2WfhfbvZA"* handling a radio emission about unfaithful women and the video having an id equal to *"_VimCUVXwaQ"* gives advices to women for becoming beautiful. Three annotators, manually review the obtained video from the keyword and manually selected 335 *video_id*. We used Youtube Data API[4] and a python script to automatically extract comments of each *video_id* and their replies. At the end, we were able to collect *373,984* comments extracted for the period between February and March 2019, we call this corpus *Corpus_Youtube_women*.

#### 4.1.2. Data annotation

For the annotation, we randomly select 5,000 comments. The annotation was done by three annotators, natives speaker of Arabic and its dialects. The annotators were separated and they had one week for manually annotated the selected comments using two labels, 1 (for hate) and 0 (for non-hate). The following points illustrate the main aspects figuring in the annotators guideline:

- The annotators should classify each comments containing injuries, hate, abusive or vulgar or offensive language against women as a comment containing hate.
- The annotators should be as objective as they can. Even if they approve the comment, they should consider it as containing hate speech is it is offensive against women.
- For having a system dealing with all type of comments, the annotators were asked to annotate all

[4]https://developers.google.com/youtube/v3/

the 5,000 comments, even if the comment speak about football or something not related to women at all. However they asked to annotate this comment with 0 and to add the label w (meaning without interest).

- When the annotators are facing a situation where they really doubt about the right label, they were asked to put the label p (for problem) rather than putting a label with which they are not convinced.

At the beginning of the annotation process, we received lots questions such as: 1) Have the hate have to be addressed to women, how to classify a message containing hate regarding men? 2) Have the hate comments absolutely contains terms indicating hate or have the annotators to handle irony?, etc. For the first question, we precise that the comments have to be addressed to women. Any others comment have to be labelled with 0 For the second question, we asked the annotators to also consider the irony and sarcasm.

After completion of the annotation process, we concentrate on the comments obtaining the same labels from all annotators. Then, we constructed two dataset. The first one (*Corpus_1*) contains 3,798 comments which are annotated with the same labels (0 or 1) from the three annotators. Among this comments 792 (which represent 20.85%) are annotated as hateful and 3006 as non-hateful. Hence, this corpus is very unbalanced. The second one (*Corpus_2*) represents the balanced version of (*Corpus_1*). For constructing this corpus, we randomly picked up 1,006 comments labelled as non-hateful and we picked up all the comments annotated as hateful. Then, we constructed a balanced corpus containing 1,798 comments.

## 4.2. Hate speech detection

### 4.2.1. Features extraction

We use two different algorithm for features extraction which are, Word2vec (Mikolov et al., 2013) and FasText (Joulin et al., 2016). We use Word2vec with classic methods and we use FasText with Deep learning methods. Word2vec describes two architectures for computing continuous vectors representations, the Skip-Gram (SG) and Continuous Bag-Of-Words (CBOW). The former predicts the context-words from a given source word, while the latter does the inverse and predicts a word given its context window (Mikolov et al., 2013). As for Word2vec, Fastext models is also based on either the skip-gram (SG) or the continuous bag-of-words (CBOW) architectures. The key difference between FastText and Word2Vec is the use of n-grams. Word2Vec learns vectors only for complete words found in the training corpus. FastText learns vectors for the n-grams that are found within each word, as well as each complete word (Joulin et al., 2016). In this work we rely on both representations of word2vec and fasText (i.e SG and CBOW).

For Word2vec model, we used the Gensim toolkit[5]. For fasText, we use the fasText library proposed by Facebook on Github[6]. For both Word2vec/fasText, we use a context of 10 words to produce representations for both CBOW and SG of length 300. We trained the Word2vec/fasText models on the corpus *Corpus_Youtube_women*

### 4.2.2. Classification

For comparing the results, we use both classification methods, classic and deep learning based. For classic method, we use five classification Algorithms such as: GaussianNB (GNB), LogisticRegression (LR), RandomForeset (RF), SGDClassifier (SGD, with loss='log' and penalty='l1') and LinearSVC (LSVC with C='1e1'). For their implementation phase, we were inspired by the classification algorithm proposed by Altowayan et al. (Altowayan and Tao, 2016). For the deep learning classification we use three models CNN, LSTM and Bi-LSTM. For each model, we use six layers. The first layer is a randomly-initialized word embedding layer that turns words in sentences into a feature map. The weights of embedding_matrix are calculated using fasText (with both SG and CBOW implementation). This layer is followed by a CNN/ LSTM/BiLSTM layer that scans the feature map (depending on the model that we defined). These layers are used with 300 filters and a width of 7, which means that each filter is trained to detect a certain pattern in a 7-gram window of words. Global maxpooling is applied to the output generated by CNN/LSTM/BiLSTM layer to take the maximum score of each pattern. The main function of the pooling layer is to reduce the dimensionality of the CNN/LSTM/BiLSTM representations by down-sampling the output and keeping the maximum value. For reducing over-fitting by preventing complex co-adaptations on training data, a Dropout layer with a probability equal to 0.5 is added. The obtained scores are then feeded to a single feed-forward (fully-connected) layer with Relu activation. Finally, the output of that layer goes through a sigmoid layer that predicts the output classes. For all the models we used Adam optimizers with epoch 100 and an early_stopping parameter for stopping the iteration in the absence of improvements.

# 5. Experimentation and Results

## 5.1. Experimental results

Table 1 presents the results obtained on *Corpus_1* and *Corpus_2*. For showing the impact of balanced/unbalanced corpus, we present the different results related to the detection of Hateful/non hateful detection separately. It can be seen from Table 1 that the F1-score obtained on unbalanced corpus (*Corpus_1*, up to 86%) are slightly better than those obtained on the balanced corpus (*Corpus_1*, up to 85%). However only

[5] https://radimrehurek.com/gensim/models/word2vec.html

[6] https://github.com/facebookresearch/fastText

Table 1: Classification results on Corpus_1

| Corpus | Models | Type | ML Alg | Hateful | | | Non-hateful | | | Average | | |
|---|---|---|---|---|---|---|---|---|---|---|---|---|
| | | | | P | R | F1 | P | R | F1 | P | R | F1 |
| | | | GNB | 0.32 | 0.80 | 0.46 | 0.91 | 0.56 | 0.69 | 0.79 | 0.61 | 0.64 |
| | | | LR | 0.70 | 0.19 | 0.30 | 0.82 | 0.98 | 0.89 | 0.80 | 0.81 | 0.77 |
| | | SG | RF | 0.69 | 0.33 | 0.44 | 0.84 | 0.96 | 0.90 | 0.81 | 0.83 | 0.80 |
| | | | SGD | 0.81 | 0.13 | 0.23 | 0.81 | 0.99 | 0.89 | 0.81 | 0.81 | 0.75 |
| | | | LSVC | 0.70 | 0.41 | 0.52 | 0.86 | 0.95 | 0.90 | 0.83 | 0.83 | 0.82 |
| | Word2vec | | | | | | | | | | | |
| | | | GNB | 0.30 | 0.82 | 0.44 | 0.91 | 0.48 | 0.63 | 0.78 | 0.55 | 0.59 |
| | | | LR | 0.75 | 0.04 | 0.07 | 0.79 | 1.00 | 0.88 | 0.79 | 0.79 | 0.71 |
| | | CBOW | RF | 0.50 | 0.17 | 0.26 | 0.81 | 0.95 | 0.88 | 0.75 | 0.79 | 0.75 |
| | | | SGD | 0.67 | 0.04 | 0.07 | 0.79 | 0.99 | 0.88 | 0.77 | 0.79 | 0.71 |
| Corpus_1 | | | LSVC | 0.57 | 0.15 | 0.24 | 0.81 | 0.97 | 0.88 | 0.76 | 0.80 | 0.75 |
| | | | CNN | 0.77 | 0.56 | **0.65** | 0.89 | 0.96 | **0.92** | 0.87 | 0.87 | **0.86** |
| | | SG | LSTM | 0.82 | 0.45 | 0.58 | 0.87 | 0.97 | 0.92 | 0.86 | 0.86 | 0.85 |
| | | | Bi-LSTM | 0.89 | 0.36 | 0.51 | 0.85 | 0.99 | 0.91 | 0.86 | 0.86 | 0.83 |
| | FasText | | | | | | | | | | | |
| | | | CNN | 0.71 | 0.46 | 0.56 | 0.87 | 0.95 | 0.91 | 0.84 | 0.85 | 0.83 |
| | | CBOW | LSTM | 0.67 | 0.53 | 0.59 | 0.88 | 0.93 | 0.90 | 0.83 | 0.84 | 0.84 |
| | | | Bi-LSTM | 0.56 | 0.61 | 0.59 | 0.89 | 0.87 | 0.88 | 0.82 | 0.82 | 0.82 |
| | | | GNB | 0.63 | 0.82 | 0.71 | 0.83 | 0.63 | 0.71 | 0.74 | 0.71 | 0.71 |
| | | | LR | 0.79 | 0.75 | 0.77 | 0.82 | 0.85 | 0.84 | 0.81 | 0.81 | 0.81 |
| | | SG | RF | 0.81 | 0.62 | 0.71 | 0.76 | 0.89 | 0.82 | 0.78 | 0.78 | 0.77 |
| | | | SGD | 0.72 | 0.85 | 0.78 | 0.87 | 0.75 | 0.81 | 0.81 | 0.79 | 0.79 |
| | | | LSVC | 0.79 | 0.74 | 0.76 | 0.81 | 0.85 | 0.83 | 0.80 | 0.80 | 0.80 |
| | Word2vec | | | | | | | | | | | |
| | | | GNB | 0.54 | 0.85 | 0.66 | 0.80 | 0.45 | 0.58 | 0.69 | 0.62 | 0.61 |
| | | | LR | 0.72 | 0.58 | 0.65 | 0.73 | 0.83 | 0.77 | 0.72 | 0.72 | 0.72 |
| | | CBOW | RF | 0.73 | 0.63 | 0.68 | 0.75 | 0.82 | 0.78 | 0.74 | 0.74 | 0.74 |
| | | | SGD | 0.77 | 0.57 | 0.65 | 0.73 | 0.87 | 0.79 | 0.74 | 0.74 | 0.73 |
| Corpus_2 | | | LSVC | 0.75 | 0.70 | 0.72 | 0.79 | 0.82 | 0.80 | 0.77 | 0.77 | 0.77 |
| | | | CNN | 0.86 | 0.69 | 0.77 | 0.80 | 0.92 | 0.85 | 0.83 | 0.82 | 0.82 |
| | | SG | LSTM | 0.93 | 0.60 | 0.73 | 0.76 | 0.97 | 0.85 | 0.83 | 0.81 | 0.80 |
| | | | Bi-LSTM | 0.85 | 0.81 | **0.83** | 0.86 | 0.89 | **0.88** | 0.85 | 0.86 | **0.85** |
| | FasText | | | | | | | | | | | |
| | | | CNN | 0.81 | 0.62 | 0.70 | 0.76 | 0.89 | 0.82 | 0.78 | 0.77 | 0.77 |
| | | SG | LSTM | 0.94 | 0.57 | 0.71 | 0.75 | 0.97 | 0.85 | 0.83 | 0.80 | 0.79 |
| | | | Bi-LSTM | 0.73 | 0.82 | 0.77 | 0.85 | 0.77 | 0.81 | 0.80 | 0.79 | 0.79 |

65% of hateful comment were correctly classified using *Corpus_1*, where 83% are correctly classified using *Corpus_2*. Deep learning classifiers (CNN, Bi-LSTM) associated to SG model of fasText outperformed other classifiers for both corpus (1 and 2). In addition SG model outperformed CBOW model for both corpus and and for all the used classifiers. It also can be observed that deep learning classifiers are more appropriate with unbalanced data (F1-score up to 65%) where the classic classifiers (GNB, LR, ect) are able to correctly classify only 52%.

## 5.2. Discussion and Analysis

The presented results are pretty good but they could be improved by integrating some pre-treatments. The first one is related to Arabizi transliteration. As Arabic people used both scripts Arabic and Arabizi. Handling them together or classifying Arabizi without calling the transliteration step could give wrong results. We previously showed that the transliteration consequently improved the results of sentiment analysis (Guellil et al., 2018a). We previously present a transliteration based on rules-based approach (Guellil et al., 2018a; Guellil et al., 2018c) but we conclude that a corpus based approach would certainly improve the results. Hence, we plan to propose a corpus-based approach for transliteration and apply this approach on the annotated corpus for having one script used for Arabic language. In addition to scripts, Arabic people also use other languages to express their opinions in social media, such as French or English. However, the proportion of these languages is not really important comparing to the proportion of Arabic and Arabizi. In the context of this study, we handle all the languages in the same corpus. However, a language identification step would consequently improve the results. Hence, as an improvement to this work, we plan to propose an identification approach between Arabizi, French and English (because they share the same script).

## 6. Conclusion

Hate speech detection is a research area attracting the research community interest more and more. Different studies have been proposed and most of them are quietly recent (during 2016 and 2019). The purpose of this studies is mitigated between the detection of hate speech in general and hate speech targeting a special community or a special group. In this context, the principal aim of this paper is to detect hate speech against women in Arabic community on social media. We automatically collected data related to women from Youtube. Afterwards, we randomly select 5,000 comments and give them to three annotators in order to labelled them as hateful or non-hateful. However, for increasing the precision, we concentrate on the portion of the corpus were all the annotators were agree. It allows us to construct a corpus containing 3,798 comments (where 3.006 are non-hateful and 792 are hateful). We also constructed a balanced corpus containing 1,798 comment randomly picked up from the aforementioned one. For validating the constructed corpus, we used different machine learning algorithm such as LSVC, GNB, SGD, etc and deep learning one such as CNN? LSTM, etc. However, The exeperimental results showed that the deep learning classifiers (especially CNN, Bi-LSTM) outperform the other classifiers by respectively achieving an F1-score up to 86%.

For improving this work we plan to integrate a transliteration system for transforming Arabizi to Arabic. We also plan to identify the different language before proceeding to the classification. Finally, we also plan to automatically increase the training corpus.

## 7. Acknowledgements

We would like to thank the Edinburgh Futures Institute (EFI)[7] for funding the fees related to the presentation of this paper. The purpose of the Edinburgh Futures Institute (EFI) is to pursue knowledge and understanding that supports the navigation of complex futures.

[7]https://efi.ed.ac.uk/

## 8. Bibliographical References

Abozinadah, E. A., Mbaziira, A. V., and Jones, J. (2015). Detection of abusive accounts with arabic tweets. *International Journal of Knowledge Engineering*, 1(2):113–119.

Al-Hassan, A. and Al-Dossari, H. (2019). Detection of hate speech in social networks: A survey on multilingual corpus. *Computer Science & Information Technology (CS & IT)*, 9(2):83.

Al-Kabi, M., Al-Ayyoub, M., Alsmadi, I., and Wahsheh, H. (2016). A prototype for a standard arabic sentiment analysis corpus. *Int. Arab J. Inf. Technol.*, 13(1A):163–170.

Alakrot, A., Murray, L., and Nikolov, N. S. (2018). Dataset construction for the detection of anti-social behaviour in online communication in arabic. *Procedia Computer Science*, 142:174–181.

Albadi, N., Kurdi, M., and Mishra, S. (2018). Are they our brothers? analysis and detection of religious hate speech in the arabic twittersphere. In *2018 IEEE/ACM International Conference on Advances in Social Networks Analysis and Mining (ASONAM)*, pages 69–76. IEEE.

Alfina, I., Mulia, R., Fanany, M. I., and Ekanata, Y. (2017). Hate speech detection in the indonesian language: A dataset and preliminary study. In *2017 International Conference on Advanced Computer Science and Information Systems (ICACSIS)*, pages 233–238. IEEE.

Altowayan, A. A. and Tao, L. (2016). Word embeddings for arabic sentiment analysis. In *Big Data (Big Data), 2016 IEEE International Conference on*, pages 3820–3825. IEEE.

Andrusyak, B., Rimel, M., and Kern, R. (2018). Detection of abusive speech for mixed sociolects of russian and ukrainian languages. *RASLAN 2018 Recent Advances in Slavonic Natural Language Processing*, page 77.

Bies, A., Song, Z., Maamouri, M., Grimes, S., Lee, H., Wright, J., Strassel, S., Habash, N., Eskander, R., and Rambow, O. (2014). Transliteration of arabizi into arabic orthography: Developing a parallel annotated arabizi-arabic script sms/chat corpus. In *Proceedings of the EMNLP 2014 Workshop on Arabic Natural Language Processing (ANLP)*, pages 93–103.

Boudad, N., Faizi, R., Thami, R. O. H., and Chiheb, R. (2017). Sentiment analysis in arabic: A review of the literature. *Ain Shams Engineering Journal*.

Burnap, P. and Williams, M. L. (2014). Hate speech, machine classification and statistical modelling of information flows on twitter: Interpretation and communication for policy decision making. pages 1–18.

Chetty, N. and Alathur, S. (2018). Hate speech review in the context of online social networks. *Aggression and violent behavior*.

Dadvar, M. and Eckert, K. (2018). Cyberbullying detection in social networks using deep learning based models; a reproducibility study. *arXiv preprint arXiv:1812.08046*.

Darwish, K. (2014). Arabizi detection and conversion to arabic. In *Proceedings of the EMNLP 2014 Workshop on Arabic Natural Language Processing (ANLP)*, pages 217–224.

Davidson, T., Warmsley, D., Macy, M., and Weber, I. (2017). Automated hate speech detection and the problem of offensive language. In *Eleventh International AAAI Conference on Web and Social Media*.

De Smedt, T., De Pauw, G., and Van Ostaeyen, P. (2018). Automatic detection of online jihadist hate speech. *arXiv preprint arXiv:1803.04596*.

Del Vigna12, F., Cimino23, A., Dell Orletta, F., Petrocchi, M., and Tesconi, M. (2017). Hate me, hate me not: Hate speech detection on facebook. In *Proceedings of the First Italian Conference on Cybersecurity (ITASEC17)*.

Eisele, A. and Chen, Y. (2010). Multiun: A multilingual corpus from united nation documents. In *LREC*.

Farghaly, A. and Shaalan, K. (2009). Arabic natural language processing: Challenges and solutions. *ACM Transactions on Asian Language Information Processing (TALIP)*, 8(4):14.

Gambäck, B. and Sikdar, U. K. (2017). Using convolutional neural networks to classify hate-speech. In *Proceedings of the first workshop on abusive language online*, pages 85–90.

Gorrell, G., Greenwood, M. A., Roberts, I., Maynard, D., and Bontcheva, K. (2018). Twits, twats and twaddle: Trends in online abuse towards uk politicians. In *Twelfth International AAAI Conference on Web and Social Media*.

Guellil, I. and Azouaou, F. (2016). Arabic dialect identification with an unsupervised learning (based on a lexicon). application case: Algerian dialect. In *Computational Science and Engineering (CSE) and IEEE Intl Conference on Embedded and Ubiquitous Computing (EUC) and 15th Intl Symposium on Distributed Computing and Applications for Business Engineering (DCABES), 2016 IEEE Intl Conference on*, pages 724–731. IEEE.

Guellil, I., Azouaou, F., and Abbas, M. (2017a). Neural vs statistical translation of algerian arabic dialect written with arabizi and arabic letter. In *The 31st Pacific Asia Conference on Language, Information and Computation PACLIC 31 (2017)*.

Guellil, I., Azouaou, F., Abbas, M., and Fatiha, S. (2017b). Arabizi transliteration of algerian arabic dialect into modern standard arabic. In *Social MT 2017: First workshop on Social Media and User Generated Content Machine Translation (co-located with EAMT 2017)*.

Guellil, I., Azouaou, F., Saâdane, H., and Semmar, N. (2017c). Une approche fondée sur les lexiques d'analyse de sentiments du dialecte algérien.

Guellil, I., Adeel, A., Azouaou, F., Benali, F., Hachani, A.-e., and Hussain, A. (2018a). Arabizi sentiment analysis based on transliteration and automatic corpus annotation. In *Proceedings of the 9th Workshop on Computational Approaches to Subjectivity, Sentiment and Social Media Analysis*, pages 335–341.

Guellil, I., Adeel, A., Azouaou, F., and Hussain, A. (2018b). Sentialg: Automated corpus annotation for algerian sentiment analysis. In *9th International Conference on Brain Inspired Cognitive Systems(BICS 2018)*.

Guellil, I., Azouaou, F., Benali, F., Hachani, a.-e., and Saadane, H. (2018c). Approche hybride pour la translitération de l'arabizi algérien : une étude préliminaire. In *Conference: 25e conférence sur le Traitement Automatique des Langues Naturelles (TALN), May 2018, Rennes, FranceAt: Rennes, France*. https://www.researchgate.net/publication ....

Guellil, I., Saâdane, H., Azouaou, F., Gueni, B., and Nouvel, D. (2019). Arabic natural language processing: An overview. *Journal of King Saud University-Computer and Information Sciences*.

Guellil, I., Azouaou, F., Benali, F., and Ala-Eddine, H. (2021). One: Toward one model, one algorithm, one corpus dedicated to sentiment analysis of arabic/arabizi and its dialects. In *Proceedings of the Eleventh Workshop on Computational Approaches to Subjectivity, Sentiment and Social Media Analysis*, pages 236–249.

Habash, N. Y. (2010). Introduction to arabic natural language processing. *Synthesis Lectures on Human Language Technologies*, 3(1):1–187.

Haidar, B., Chamoun, M., and Serhrouchni, A. (2017). A multilingual system for cyberbullying detection: Arabic content detection using machine learning. *Advances in Science, Technology and Engineering Systems Journal*, 2(6):275–284.

Harrat, S., Meftouh, K., and Smaïli, K. (2017). Maghrebi arabic dialect processing: an overview. In *ICNLSSP 2017-International Conference on Natural Language, Signal and Speech Processing*.

Imane, G., Kareem, D., and Faical, A. (2019). A set of parameters for automatically annotating a sentiment arabic corpus. *International Journal of Web Information Systems*.

Joulin, A., Grave, E., Bojanowski, P., and Mikolov, T. (2016). Bag of tricks for efficient text classification. *arXiv preprint arXiv:1607.01759*.

Kallas, P. (2017). Top 15 most popular social networking sites and apps. *Consultado em Setembro*, 20:2017.

Köffer, S., Riehle, D. M., Höhenberger, S., and Becker, J. (2018). Discussing the value of automatic hate speech detection in online debates. *Multikonferenz*

*Wirtschaftsinformatik (MKWI 2018): Data Driven X-Turning Data in Value, Leuphana, Germany*.

Kshirsagar, R., Cukuvac, T., McKeown, K., and McGregor, S. (2018). Predictive embeddings for hate speech detection on twitter. *arXiv preprint arXiv:1809.10644*.

Madisetty, S. and Desarkar, M. S. (2018). Aggression detection in social media using deep neural networks. In *Proceedings of the First Workshop on Trolling, Aggression and Cyberbullying (TRAC-2018)*, pages 120–127.

Mikolov, T., Chen, K., Corrado, G., and Dean, J. (2013). Efficient estimation of word representations in vector space. *arXiv preprint arXiv:1301.3781*.

Mubarak, H., Darwish, K., and Magdy, W. (2017). Abusive language detection on arabic social media. In *Proceedings of the First Workshop on Abusive Language Online*, pages 52–56.

Nockleby, J. T. (2000). Hate speech. *Encyclopedia of the American constitution*, 3(2):1277–1279.

Park, J. H. and Fung, P. (2017). One-step and two-step classification for abusive language detection on twitter. *arXiv preprint arXiv:1706.01206*.

Pitsilis, G. K., Ramampiaro, H., and Langseth, H. (2018). Detecting offensive language in tweets using deep learning. *arXiv preprint arXiv:1801.04433*.

Puiu, A.-B. and Brabete, A.-O. (2019). Semeval-2019 task 6: Identifying and categorizing offensive language in social media. *arXiv preprint arXiv:1903.00665*.

Razavi, A. H., Inkpen, D., Uritsky, S., and Matwin, S. (2010). Offensive language detection using multi-level classification. In *Canadian Conference on Artificial Intelligence*, pages 16–27. Springer.

Risch, J., Krebs, E., Löser, A., Riese, A., and Krestel, R. (2018). Fine-grained classification of offensive language. In *14th Conference on Natural Language Processing KONVENS 2018*.

Saha, P., Mathew, B., Goyal, P., and Mukherjee, A. (2018). Hateminers: Detecting hate speech against women. *arXiv preprint arXiv:1812.06700*.

Schmidt, A. and Wiegand, M. (2017). A survey on hate speech detection using natural language processing. In *Proceedings of the Fifth International Workshop on Natural Language Processing for Social Media*, pages 1–10.

Sharaf, A.-B. M. and Atwell, E. (2012a). Qurana: Corpus of the quran annotated with pronominal anaphora. In *LREC*. Citeseer.

Sharaf, A.-B. M. and Atwell, E. (2012b). Qursim: A corpus for evaluation of relatedness in short texts. In *LREC*, pages 2295–2302.

Soliman, A. B., Eissa, K., and El-Beltagy, S. R. (2017). Aravec: A set of arabic word embedding models for use in arabic nlp. *Procedia Computer Science*, 117:256–265.

Van Hee, C., Jacobs, G., Emmery, C., Desmet, B., Lefever, E., Verhoeven, B., De Pauw, G., Daelemans, W., and Hoste, V. (2018). Automatic detection of cyberbullying in social media text. *PloS one*, 13(10):e0203794.

Warner, W. and Hirschberg, J. (2012). Detecting hate speech on the world wide web. In *Proceedings of the Second Workshop on Language in Social Media*, pages 19–26. Association for Computational Linguistics.

Waseem, Z. and Hovy, D. (2016). Hateful symbols or hateful people? predictive features for hate speech detection on twitter. In *Proceedings of the NAACL student research workshop*, pages 88–93.

Waseem, Z. (2016). Are you a racist or am i seeing things? annotator influence on hate speech detection on twitter. In *Proceedings of the first workshop on NLP and computational social science*, pages 138–142.

Wiegand, M., Ruppenhofer, J., Schmidt, A., and Greenberg, C. (2018). Inducing a lexicon of abusive words–a feature-based approach. pages 1046–1056.

Zhang, Z. and Luo, L. (2018). Hate speech detection: A solved problem? the challenging case of long tail on twitter. *Semantic Web*, (Preprint):1–21.

Zhang, Z., Robinson, D., and Tepper, J. (2018). Detecting hate speech on twitter using a convolution-gru based deep neural network. In *European Semantic Web Conference*, pages 745–760. Springer.

Ziemski, M., Junczys-Dowmunt, M., and Pouliquen, B. (2016). The united nations parallel corpus v1. 0. In *LREC*.

*Proceedings of the 1st Workshop on Dataset Creation for Lower-Resourced Languages (DCLRL) @LREC2022*, pages 76–82
Marseille, 24 June 2022


# Word-level Language Identification Using Subword Embeddings for Code-mixed Bangla-English Social Media Data

**Aparna Dutta**
Brandeis University
415 South St, Waltham, MA 02453, United States
aparnadutta@brandeis.edu

**Abstract**

This paper reports work on building a word-level language identification (LID) model for code-mixed Bangla-English social media data using subword embeddings, with an ultimate goal of using this LID module as the first step in a modular part-of-speech (POS) tagger in future research. This work reports preliminary results of a word-level LID model that uses a single bidirectional LSTM with subword embeddings trained on very limited code-mixed resources. At the time of writing, there are no previous reported results available in which subword embeddings are used for language identification with the Bangla-English code-mixed language pair. As part of the current work, a labeled resource for word-level language identification is also presented, by correcting 85.7% of labels from the 2016 ICON Whatsapp Bangla-English dataset (ICON, 2016). The trained model was evaluated on a test set of 4,015 tokens compiled from the 2015 and 2016 ICON datasets, and achieved a test accuracy of 93.61%.

**Keywords:** Bangla, Bengali, code-mixing, code-switching, language identification, subword embeddings

## 1. Introduction

Code-mixing refers to the phenomenon to communication using two or more languages interchangeably within the same phrase, and is widely-observed in areas with significant multilingual populations. India has 22 official native languages, but its usage of English also contributes to its linguistic diversity. English has widespread usage in India in both informal and official contexts, with it being the main language used in schools and educational contexts. Bilingualism is very common in India and people are accustomed to speaking in a mix of English and other Indian languages.

Bangla is the second most-spoken native language in India and is frequently mixed with English and Hindi on social media, as code-mixing is particularly common in social media communication. Although Bangla and Hindi each have their own native scripts with accompanying digital keyboards, speakers often switch between multiple languages within one social media post, and it is more convenient to transliterate into Roman characters than to switch back and forth between keyboards.

The automatic understanding of social media text has become a key research area in recent years, and being able to identify the language for individual words in code-mixed text is a prerequisite for more complex downstream NLP tasks such as part-of-speech (POS) tagging, named entity recognition, and sentiment analysis. In many cases, language identification can allow the reuse of existing monolingual models rather than re-training models for each new code-mixed language pair. For this reason, one of the foundational problems for NLP with code-mixed data is language identification at the word level.

This paper's main contribution is providing baseline results for a Bangla-English word-level LID model with subword embeddings, using very limited data and no external resources. Although subword embeddings have been used for language identification with other code-mixed language pairs, there are no reported results of subword embeddings applied to Bangla-English code-mixing to the best of our knowledge.

The next section discusses specific challenges of language identification with Bangla-English social media data. Section 3 then describes the dataset that was used for training and evaluating the model. The methodology used for word-level language identification is discussed in section 4, and the results are reported and discussed in section 5. Finally, section 6 wraps up the overall findings of the paper and suggests a future direction for this research. **Reproducibility:** Source code and data are available at: `https://github.com/aparnadutta/code-mixed-lid`.

## 2. Related Work

This section provides an overview of past research into word-level LID for code-mixed data, focusing on the Bangla-English code-mixed pair.

Research into language identification for code-mixed data first began with Solorio and Liu (2008)'s initial research into predicting code-switching points. Solorio and Liu's work used a spoken Spanish-English corpus and tested both Naive Bayes and VF1 (Value Feature Interval) models. They found that Naive Bayes performed best, gaining an F1-score of 28%.

Das and Gambäck (2014) introduced the first Indian social media text corpus for the task of language-identification, and achieved an F1-score of 76.37% on Bangla-English, using an SVM trained with ngrams with weights, dictionary, minimum edit distance, and a 7-word context window. In this research, Das and Gambäck also introduce the code-mixing index (CMI) to evaluate the level of code-mixing across corpora. This is a metric used to quantify the amount of code-mixing that is present in a corpus, and can allow researchers to better compare results using different corpora.

One of the most well-known approaches to word-level language identification for code-mixed data was conducted by Sristy et al. (2017). Their best-performing Bangla-English model achieved an F1-score of 86.15% using Naive Bayes EM with CRF (Lafferty et al., 2001).

Barman et al. (2014) reported one of the highest metrics on the task of word-level language identification, with an accuracy 95.14% using a CRF model. However, they excluded named entities and word-level mixing from their training and test sets. They also noted that there was a substantial token-level overlap between their cross-validation and test sets, such that their baseline dictionary approach already achieves an accuracy of 93.65%. This makes it difficult to compare these results to other studies that include these more difficult to handle labels in their testing sets.

More recently, advanced deep-learning approaches have proven to be very successful at the task of word-level LID. Jamatia et al. (2019) compared the performance of CRFs to LSTMs (long short term memory) and BiLSTMs (bidirectional long short term memory) (Huang et al., 2015), both deep-learning based approaches. Their research utilized a Bangla-English corpus, and is most similar to the dataset being used in the current work. They found that the LSTM and BiLSTM significantly outperformed the baseline CRF (81.57% F1 and 83.93% accuracy) on the Bangla-English data, with a slight improvement between the LSTM (88.19% F1 and 88.27% accuracy) and BiLSTM (88.23% F1 and 87.57% accuracy) approaches.

LSTMs and BiLSTMs have shown to be successful at this task because they are able to capture contextual relationships and long-distance dependencies between words. The next section details various input representations that have been explored for LSTMs, along with their benefits and drawbacks.

## 2.1. Input Representations for LSTMs

Word-level, character level, concatenated word and character, and more recently subword embeddings have been used as input representations for LSTMs. Each of these embedding levels indicates the granularity that is be used to map a given sentence into a group of embeddings.

### 2.1.1. Word embeddings

Word embeddings are considered the default input representations for text processing due to their logical nature, but are more likely to encounter out-of-vocabulary (OOV) issues when faced with unknown words, or noisy or misspelled data. These are dense representations of words that exhibit similarity between words with similar meanings or contexts. When an unknown word is encountered in a word-based representation, it is by default mapped to the embedding for an unknown token, leaving the neural network to rely on only the contextual information from surrounding words. As mentioned earlier, Jamatia et al. (2019) used word embeddings with LSTMs on Bangla-English data and trained their embeddings on both code-mixed social media data and monolingual Wikipedia data, achieving an F1-score of 88.23%.

### 2.1.2. Character embeddings

An alternate input representation that is used to address the OOV problem present with word embeddings is the character-level embedding. Character embeddings are generated on a character-by-character basis, and then pooled using a CNN (convolutional neural network) (Kim, 2014) to achieve word-level representations. The pooling layer prevents misspellings and abbreviations from causing OOV problems. Pooled character embeddings can either be used alone or concatenated to the original word embeddings to capture additional context and make up for OOV tokens and noisy data.

Mandal et al. (2018) used character embeddings along with phonetic-based character embeddings with an LSTM to build an ensemble model for language tagging. Their phonetic model alone achieved the best results, with an F1-score of 91.71% on Bangla-English code-mixing, but they also explored an ensemble threshold model that took the mean of the outputs of both models and used a brute force technique to select between the two. With this ensemble model they achieved an F1-score of 92.35%. However, they discarded all words with lengths less than 3, numeric characters, or word-level mixing from their training and test datasets. These adjustments make the task less transferable to data in the wild, and less comparable to the current study since this noisier data is included in the present study. Additionally, the ensemble model that performed best requires two different models to be trained, which is complex and computationally expensive.

### 2.1.3. Subword embeddings

The final input representation explored here is subword embeddings. A subword is a unit smaller than a word but larger than a character. Subwords can be generated through multiple approaches including unigram and byte-pair encoding (BPE), but in general, result in a vocabulary consisting of character groupings that appear most commonly in the data. This type of representation falls in between word-level and character-level embedding and can be especially useful for code-mixed data because unknown words will be broken into smaller subwords until they can be recognized by the vocabulary, while more common words and affixes can be recognized and build up individual embedding representations over time.

More recently, Joshi and Joshi (2021) evaluated word, character, and subword level representations for language identification in Hindi-English code-mixed data. They experimented with CNN, multi-CNN, BiLSTM, CNN+BiLSTM, and character CNN+BiLSTM models, each with word-level and subword-level input. They found that word embeddings performed worst, with word+character embeddings performing slightly better. Across all combinations, the plain BiLSTM model with the subword input representation performed best, with F1-scores of 95.64% and 92.60% for English and Hindi respectively.

By comparing all input representations, Joshi and Joshi showed that subword embeddings work remarkably well for code-mixed social media data by vastly reducing the number of OOV tokens, because the vocabulary is specifically broken into the most common chunks. While their results show the success of subword embeddings on the task of language identification with Hindi-English data, this is an area yet to be explored within the Bangla-English code-mixing literature. With this motivation for the current task, the next section will describe some particular challenges of dealing with code-mixed Bangla-English data.

## 3. Challenges of Bangla-English Language Identification

This section introduces some of the challenges that were encountered during the development of the system, specifically with respect to the data.

**Transliteration** is one of the main challenges of code-mixed Bangla-English data. Although there are formalized systems for transliterating Bangla into Roman or Latin script such as IAST (International Alphabet of Sanskrit Transliteration) and ITRANS (Indian languages Transliteration), these have not been widely adopted by social media users. Additionally, conversion from Bangla into Roman script is not one-to-one, since Bangla has more sounds than English, and even traditional Bangla orthography does not accurately reflect pronunciation due to its strict adherence to the Sanskrit writing system. All of these issues result in the same word often being transliterated in multiple different ways by social media users. For example, the Bangla word *shaathey* meaning 'together', is also transliterated as *sathei* and *shatey* within the data.

**Language ambiguous words** are also common in the data. There are many words between Bangla and English that appear orthographically identical, such as *to* meaning 'so', *choke* meaning 'eyes', and *dish* meaning 'give' in Bangla. In these cases, the text of the word itself cannot be used to identify the language of the token, as the word would be broken into the same subwords and mapped to the same embedding spaces. Instead, a more accurate language classification would rely wholly on the context of the surrounding words and the grammatical structure of the sentence.

One final difficulty is caused by **abbreviations and misspellings**. Some examples of this are *ka6e* used for *kachey* (meaning 'near'), *hbe* for *hobe* (meaning 'it will happen'), and *j* for *jey* (meaning 'that'). The shortening of words in this way can make it extremely difficult to figure out the language of a token, especially when there are English abbreviations that may have the same form. Similarly, words on social media are often misspelled, both accidentally and on purpose for exaggeration or effect, in cases like 'plssssssss' and *vishoooon* meaning 'very'.

Overall, transliteration is noisy, as social media users use shorter length words and incorporate more abbreviations than are present in standard text. These issues can all lead to OOV errors (when the system sees a new word it hasn't previously encountered) and make it more difficult to complete language identification. The next section goes into more detail on the dataset used for training and testing the model, along with any pre-processing that has been done to address the challenges mentioned here.

## 4. Dataset

The dataset used for training, development, and evaluation of the model was compiled from the 2015 and 2016 ICON shared tasks. Although both corpora consist primarily of Bangla-English code-mixing, there are also Hindi words present in the data. For both shared tasks, the training data was publicly released online[1] but the validation and testing sets were not made publicly available.

The 2016 ICON data consists of English-Bangla code-mixed data that was scraped from Facebook, Twitter, and WhatsApp, and was manually and automatically tagged at the word level. The 2015 data also consists of social media data, but is not broken into separate files based on source. For the current research, only the word-level language tags are used.

### 4.1. Data Correction and Pre-processing

The language tags in the 2016 WhatsApp dataset were manually corrected for the purposes of this research. A large majority of the tokens that were clearly Bangla or English were originally mis-labeled as *undef* or *univ* in this dataset. As such, 85.7% of the original language tags were manually corrected by a native speaker of Bangla and English, with a background in linguistics and annotation. The tags in the Facebook and Twitter datasets were also examined but did not appear to have these issues. The corrected dataset is released with this project for future usage.

The data was also minimally pre-processed to address the challenges described in the previous section. All words were lowercased, and words with ¿2 consecutive identical characters were normalized to 2 consecutive characters (Mandal et al., 2018). Finally, la-

[1] http://www.amitavadas.com/Code-Mixing.html

bels for words that included word-level mixing such as *en+bn_suffix* or *be+en_suffix* were collapsed into a single *mixed* label because there were too few examples of word-level mixing in the data to enable accurate classification.

### 4.2. Language Tag Breakdown

Table 1 shows the token-level distribution of languages from each data source. The Facebook, Twitter and WhatsApp sources are come from the 2016 data, while the 2015 data is grouped together into one source. The 2015 data makes up over half of the tokens in the overall dataset, and is also the only source that is majority English rather than Bangla. For a more in-depth comparison of the various sources, the code-mixing index of the dataset is discussed next.

### 4.3. Code-mixing Index

CMI is a metric that was introduced by Das and Gambäck (2014) to measure the amount of code-mixing present in a corpus. This is a useful metric because it allows researchers to understand when results are comparable from research using different code-mixed datasets. Since some corpora may contain monolingual sentences as well as code-mixed sentences, the CMI of a test dataset can also be used to evaluate the performance of the tool on different real-world cases. CMI is calculated for each utterance using the following formula:

$$CMI = \begin{cases} 100 \times [1 - \frac{max\{w_i\}}{n-u}] & : n > u \\ 0 & : n = u \end{cases}$$

Where $w_i$ is the words tagged with a language tag such as: $bn, en, hi, mixed$, while excluding non-language tags such as $univ, acro, ne, undef$. Therefore, $max_w i$ refers to the count of the most common language tag in the post. So, a monolingual utterance of Bangla would have a CMI of 0, since the number of Bangla tokens would be equal to the number of overall language tokens minus the number of non-language tokens. Similarly, a post with only non-language tokens would also have a CMI of 0.

The CMI of each data source is presented here in Table 3. The 'all' column describes the average utterance-level CMI for all utterances in the dataset, while 'mixed' refers to the average utterance-level CMI for utterances that have any code-mixing at all. This provides a better picture of the amount of code-mixing at the utterance-level. Finally, the last column shows the percentage of overall utterances from each dataset that are at all code-mixed, meaning utterances that have a non-zero CMI. The 2015 dataset exhibits far less code-mixing than the 2016 sources, which are almost entirely code-mixed.

Since the datasets are significantly different from one another in terms of code-mixing and the majority of the data comes from ICON 2015, the decision was made to shuffle the full dataset and then divide it into train, validation, and test splits using a 60%: 20%: 20% ratio. This allowed us to have a final dataset that is not entirely code-mixed or monolingual. However, this also means that there is a risk of overfitting since the test data may be too similar to the training and validation data. In order to address this concern, the overlap in tokens between the validation and test sets is reported here, as per Barman et al. (2014). 33.47% of the Bangla tokens in the test set were also present in the validation set, while 40.73% of the English tokens in the test set were also present in the validation set. This is significantly less overlap than was reported by Barman et al., and is adequate for the current purposes.

## 5. System Design

This section describes the architecture of the model built for Bangla-English word-level language identification. The task of language identification in code-mixed text can be defined as a joint sequence-labeling and classification task. The language of each word in a given utterance must be individually labeled, but incorporating the context of surrounding words is also crucially important to account for challenges like orthographic similarity between words of different languages, and out-of-vocabulary tokens.

To address these challenges, a BiLSTM model is used following Joshi and Joshi (2021)'s experimental setup, with modifications made to account for a smaller dataset with more labels. The dataset used by Joshi and Joshi contained only Hindi and English language labels and was a binary task, while the current dataset contains at least three languages (Bangla, English, and Hindi) as well as mixed language labels, making the current task a problem of multiclass classification. To address the multiclass problem, a softmax activation is used rather than a sigmoid activation in the current work.

Figure 1 shows a general architecture of the full model with the sentence *toder college ta* meaning *'your college'* being split into subwords. Each subword embedding passes through the model to generate the final output. The model is a single-layer BiLSTM that uses unigram-based subword embeddings as the input representation.

### 5.1. Vocab Generation Using SentencePiece

The first step in the task involves generating an embedding vocabulary for the text input. Following Joshi and Joshi (2021), the subword model is trained using Google SentencePiece (Kudo and Richardson, 2018)[2]. All of the unlabeled training data is used to train the SentencePiece model, which is then able to split each word in a sentence into smaller subwords.

The subword vocab size used by Joshi and Joshi (2021) was 12k tokens, but due to the smaller amount of avail-

[2]https://github.com/google/sentencepiece

| Source | # | Language Label | | | | | | | |
|---|---|---|---|---|---|---|---|---|---|
| | tokens | bn | en | univ | ne | acro | hi | mixed | undef |
| Facebook 2016 | 7,392 | 48.55 | 29.76 | 17.06 | 2.91 | 0.54 | 1.16 | 0.00 | 0.01 |
| Twitter 2016 | 3,680 | 48.72 | 26.60 | 19.84 | 2.99 | 0.27 | 0.68 | 0.22 | 0.68 |
| WhatsApp 2016 | 3,510 | 52.99 | 34.25 | 10.11 | 2.28 | 0.00 | 0.14 | 0.09 | 0.14 |
| ICON 2015 | 24,547 | 33.94 | 40.60 | 19.03 | 2.80 | 2.51 | 0.80 | 0.19 | 0.12 |
| Total | 39,129 | 39.80 | 36.67 | 17.94 | 2.79 | 1.70 | 0.80 | 0.15 | 0.16 |

Table 1: Token-level language distribution from all sources (%). The language tags are Bangla, English, Universal (punctuation and numbers), Named Entity, Acronym, Hindi, Mixed (word in one language and suffix in another), and Undefined (things that can't be classified, or non-Unicode).

| Source | Number of | | CMI | | Code-mixed |
|---|---|---|---|---|---|
| | tokens | utterances | all | mixed | (%) |
| Facebook 2016 | 7,392 | 147 | 31.63 | 31.63 | 100.00 |
| Twitter 2016 | 3,680 | 172 | 33.50 | 33.50 | 100.00 |
| WhatsApp 2016 | 3,510 | 304 | 28.17 | 29.63 | 95.07 |
| ICON 2015 | 24,547 | 2,828 | 4.88 | 25.14 | 19.41 |
| Total | 39,129 | 3,451 | 9.50 | 28.33 | 33.53 |

Table 2: Average Code-Mixing Index (CMI) for all data sources

able data for the current work, a vocab size of 3k tokens was chosen. The final model is tested using both a unigram and BPE based subword tokenizer.

The next step after generating the subword vocabulary is to complete the language identification task using the BiLSTM, as is described in the next section.

### 5.2. Sequence Labeling Using BiLSTM

This section describes the step-by-step sequence labeling task for word-level language identification, as illustrated in Figure 1. This details all of the steps involved in outputting the final tagged sentence at the word level.

1. Model input is a single social media post (or utterance). The full utterance is segmented into a flat list of subwords.
2. Each subword is mapped to an index, which is later used to retrieve embeddings. Embeddings are initialized randomly and trained over time.
3. Each subword embedding (representing one timestep) passes through the BiLSTM recurrent unit. The first subword of each token is assigned the real language label while the remaining subwords are assigned a dummy label. Masks are created to track the indices of the first subword of each token.
4. The hidden state of the recurrent unit after reading all of the subwords is used as input to a dense layer, which outputs features of shape $(S, V)$, with $S$ being the number of subwords in the utterance, and $V$ being the number of possible language tags.
5. A softmax activation function is applied to the resulting scores which results in a probability distribution over all possible language labels for each subword.
6. During training, dummy labels for non-initial subwords are masked from cross-entropy loss calculations. Predictions are generated for only the first subword in each token. This is accomplished by predicting a label for each subword, and masking the non-initial subwords so that the length of the final predictions made is equal to the number of original tokens in the utterance.
7. The argmax of the masked scores is taken for each word, resulting in a single language prediction for each original word in the sentence.

The implementation of the steps described above can be found here[3]

## 6. Evaluation

The system was evaluated using precision, recall, and F1-score, on 20% of the data set aside before training. The hyperparameters selected follow Joshi and Joshi (2021)'s work on Hindi-English code-mixed data as closely as possible, with the only change being a reduced subword vocab size due to the lack of data. The results on the validation set were used to determine the optimal number of epochs for running.

The recurrent unit has a hidden dimension of 300. The subword embedding dimension is 300, and is passed through the recurrent unit after a dropout (Srivastava et al., 2014) of 0.4 . The output of the recurrent unit is passed through one dense layer, with the final output dimension being equal to the number of language labels. An AdamW optimizer (Loshchilov and Hutter, 2017) is used and the loss function is cross-entropy with the dummy label index ignored. The model is trained for

[3]https://github.com/aparnadutta/code-mixed-lid/tree/main/src

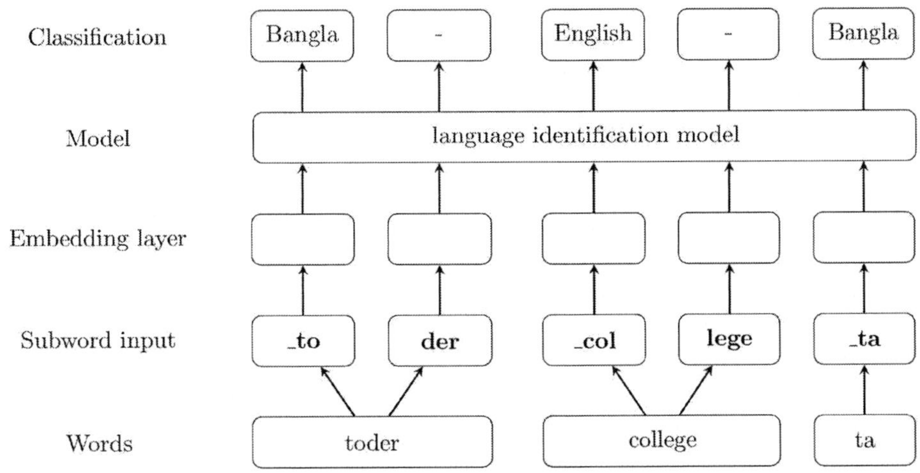


Figure 1: Outline of subword embedding language identification module using a single layer BiLSTM

| Subword Model | Metric (%) | bn | en | univ | ne | hi | acro | mixed | undef |
|---|---|---|---|---|---|---|---|---|---|
| Unigram | Precision | 92.99 | 93.27 | 98.07 | 61.17 | 79.12 | 48.81 | 25.00 | 37.50 |
| | Recall | 94.58 | 93.83 | 98.37 | 45.63 | 60.00 | 64.06 | 18.18 | 75.00 |
| | F1-Score | **93.78** | **93.56** | 98.22 | 52.27 | 68.25 | 55.41 | 21.05 | 50.00 |
| BPE | Precision | 91.60 | 93.89 | 98.21 | 62.31 | 59.83 | 56.72 | 27.27 | 100.00 |
| | Recall | 94.58 | 92.73 | 97.62 | 49.21 | 58.33 | 59.38 | 27.27 | 75.00 |
| | F1-Score | **93.07** | **93.31** | 97.91 | 54.99 | 59.07 | 58.02 | 27.27 | 85.71 |

Table 3: Metrics on test data with unigram and BPE-based subword encodings (%)

40 epochs with a batch size of 64. The same hyper-parameters are used when evaluating both unigram and BPE encoding on the test set.

### 6.1. Results and Discussion

To understand the effect of both subword encoding models, the final trained model tuned on the validation set was evaluated on a blind test set, consisting of 20% of the overall dataset. The results on the test set for both the unigram and BPE models are provided in Table 2.

The performance achieved by the model on the test set is comparable to that of previously best-performing models. The unigram model performed best, achieving F1-scores of 93.22% and 93.56% on Bangla and English respectively. The unigram and BPE-based encodings performed very similarly to one another. Due to the nature of the model training and encoding, it is not possible to say whether or not this difference is statistically significant. This is because re-training the SentencePiece model with the same encoding multiple times results in a slightly different vocabulary each time.

Looking back to past research, Mandal et al. (2018) best ensemble model achieved an F1-score of 92.35%, but it is difficult to compare the present results to other works since they have been tested on different datasets that have varying amounts of code-mixing. Regardless, the F1-scores exhibited by the unigram model are very good within the landscape, and it would be worthwhile gain access to an existing test set to re-test the fully trained model.

## 7. Ethical Considerations and Broader Impact

The main impact of this work is that of providing a large corrected dataset of code-mixed Bangla-English data. The usage of an incorrectly labeled dataset can in many ways hinder the progress of research for lower-resourced languages. This corrected data will allow further research into Bangla-English code-mixing, and will also enable us as a research community to understand a wider variety of people through their language use.

## 8. Conclusion

The first section of this paper introduced code-mixed social media data and the various approaches that have been taken to it in the past. Then, the importance of word-level language identification was discussed with a description of various input representations, ending with Joshi and Joshi (2021) findings that subword embeddings are the best-performing input representation for language identification on Hindi-English code mixed data.

After this, section 3 described the features of the ICON 2016 dataset that were used for building the LID module and evaluation of the entire model. In section 4, the overall model architecture was described, followed by the results of each experiment in section 5. The major findings were that subword embeddings perform very well on Bangla-English with F1-scores of 93.22% and 93.56% for Bangla and English respectively. While it is difficult to compare directly with previous studies due to differences in code-mixed corpora and test sets, these results are very promising given the simplicity of the current model.

In the future, it would be worthwhile to explore how mixed-language labels can be better handled. As mentioned, in the current research all mixed-language labels are collapsed into one category due to the small number present in the data. However, with a larger dataset, it would be interesting to experiment with collapsing word-level mixes into one of the two categories present in the mixing, or to keep them as their own category. Another future direction of the work is exploring other strategies for combining subword predictions for each word. In the current work, Joshi and Joshi (2021)'s approach of assigning a dummy label to and masking out non-initial subwords is used. One approach that could be explored in the future is assigning the parent label to all subwords, and utilizing masking in a different way to combine all subwords back into one parent label.

## 9. Bibliographical References


Barman, U., Das, A., Wagner, J., and Foster, J. (2014). Code mixing: A challenge for language identification in the language of social media. In *Proceedings of the First Workshop on Computational Approaches to Code Switching*, pages 13–23, Doha, Qatar, October. Association for Computational Linguistics.

Das, A. and Gambäck, B. (2013). Code-mixing in social media text. the last language identification frontier? *Trait. Autom. des Langues*, 54:41–64.

Das, A. and Gambäck, B. (2014). Identifying languages at the word level in code-mixed Indian social media text. In *Proceedings of the 11th International Conference on Natural Language Processing*, pages 378–387, Goa, India, December. NLP Association of India.

Huang, Z., Xu, W., and Yu, K. (2015). Bidirectional LSTM-CRF models for sequence tagging. *CoRR*, abs/1508.01991.

ICON. (2016). Icon 2016: Iit (bhu), varanasi ltrc, iiit, hyderabad.

Jamatia, A., Das, A., and Gambäck, B. (2019). Deep learning-based language identification in english-hindi-bengali code-mixed social media corpora. *Journal of Intelligent Systems*, 28:399 – 408.

Joshi, R. and Joshi, R. (2021). Evaluating input representation for language identification in hindi-english code mixed text. In *Lecture Notes in Electrical Engineering*, pages 795–802. Springer Singapore, nov.

Kim, Y. (2014). Convolutional neural networks for sentence classification.

Kudo, T. and Richardson, J. (2018). Sentencepiece: A simple and language independent subword tokenizer and detokenizer for neural text processing.

Lafferty, J. D., McCallum, A., and Pereira, F. C. N. (2001). Conditional random fields: Probabilistic models for segmenting and labeling sequence data. In *Proceedings of the Eighteenth International Conference on Machine Learning*, ICML '01, pages 282–289, San Francisco, CA, USA. Morgan Kaufmann Publishers Inc.

Loshchilov, I. and Hutter, F. (2017). Decoupled weight decay regularization.

Mandal, S., Das, S. D., and Das, D. (2018). Language identification of bengali-english code-mixed data using character & phonetic based LSTM models. *CoRR*, abs/1803.03859.

Solorio, T. and Liu, Y. (2008). Learning to predict code-switching points. In *Proceedings of the 2008 Conference on Empirical Methods in Natural Language Processing*, pages 973–981, Honolulu, Hawaii, October. Association for Computational Linguistics.

Sristy, N. B., Krishna, N. S., Krishna, B. S., and Ravi, V. (2017). Language identification in mixed script. In *Proceedings of the 9th Annual Meeting of the Forum for Information Retrieval Evaluation*, FIRE'17, page 14–20, New York, NY, USA. Association for Computing Machinery.

Srivastava, N., Hinton, G., Krizhevsky, A., Sutskever, I., and Salakhutdinov, R. (2014). Dropout: A simple way to prevent neural networks from overfitting. *J. Mach. Learn. Res.*, 15(1):1929–1958, jan.

# Author Index

**Association for Computational Linguistics**
209 N. Eighth Street
Stroudsburg, Pennsylvania 18360

ISBN 978-1-7138-6117-1

9 781713 861171

CURRAN ASSOCIATES INC.
proceedings.com